Paper Crafting Beautiful
Boxes, Book Covers
& Frames

Editor: Cristina Sperandeo
Photography: Alberto Bertoldi and Mario Matteucci
Translation: Chiara Tarsia
Graphic design and layout: Paola Maserra and Amelia Verga

Library of Congress Cataloging-in-Publication Data Available

10 9 8 7 6 5 4 3 2 1

Published by Sterling Publishing Company, Inc.
387 Park Avenue South, New York, N.Y. 10016
Originally published in Italy and © 1997 by RCS Libri & Grandi Opere S.p.a., Milan
under the title *Manuale di Cartonaggio*
English translation © 1999 by Sterling Publishing
Distributed in Canada by Sterling Publishing
%o Canadian Manda Group, One Atlantic Avenue, Suite 105
Toronto, Ontario, Canada M6K 3E7
Distributed in Great Britain and Europe by Cassell PLC
Wellington House, 125 Strand, London WC2R 0BB, England
Distributed in Australia by Capricorn Link (Australia) Pty Ltd.
P.O. Box 6651, Baulkham Hills, Business Centre, NSW 2153, Australia

Sterling ISBN 0-8069-9953-5

Paper Crafting Beautiful BOXES, BOOK COVERS & FRAMES

Valeria Ferrari & Ersilia Fiorucci

Sterling Publishing Co., Inc.
New York

CONTENTS

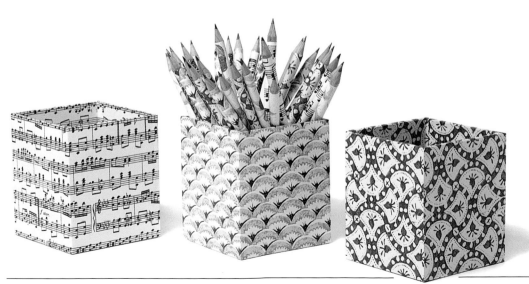

PROJECTS 27

IDEAS 135

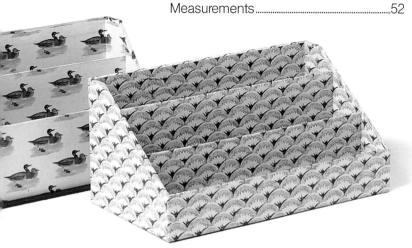

BASICS

This book is intended to be a step-by-step course in paper crafting, something we have been teaching to adults who generally have no prior experience. If you are a beginner, we recommend that you read the entire Basics section (pages 8–25) so that you will know what you are getting into. Don't worry if you can't remember it all at once. All of the project instructions are furnished for you as well as the how-to's of individual techniques. If you work the projects step by step and in the order they appear in the book, your skills will build progressively as you go. If you prefer to design your own projects, you can learn the techniques in this book and then let your creativity take over. Even if you are an old hand at paper crafting, you may still find some new tips and tricks in this book that will enhance your work. We hope you will spend many pleasant hours enjoying paper crafting.

Valeria and Ersilia

MATERIALS

PAPER

It is the paper that provides the main decoration on paper craft items. It is through your choice of papers that you express your personal taste. There are, however, some practical considerations that help determine the choice of paper and that are important for successful results, such as the holding power or consistency of the glue. Many types of paper are available, ranging from exquisite hand-painted ones with their marble or peacock designs through the silky moire patterns down to the most simple plain types. All give excellent results, though some are more difficult to work with than others. New products are constantly being developed and it is best to test them beforehand when using them for the first time. Almost all the types of paper listed below are available in bookbinding supply stores. They can also be found in stationery and crafts stores. A short list of the chief categories of paper follows, along with their main characteristics.

VARESE PAPER

This is the most suitable type of paper for paper crafting work and we recommend beginning with it, if possible. It offers a wide range of designs and colors, is of a good consistency, and holds glue well. It does not let the color of the base show through and is, therefore, easy to use. It measures about 28" x 18" per sheet.

SILKY PAPER

This is a delicate paper suitable for small, infrequently handled items. It is thin, difficult to glue, and ribbons and fabrics tend to show through slightly. If rubbed while moist this paper will more than likely lose its color.

GLOSSY PAPER

This paper is thinner than the Varese type. The glossy or slick side does not allow air to filter through. With this paper it is more difficult to gauge the amount of glue, which will dry more slowly, increasing the risk of air bubbles forming.

HANDMADE PAPER

This is the most expensive type of paper. Even today sheets of most handmade paper are one of a kind. This paper is thicker and stiffer than the others, so it is more difficult to use when folding to make angles and corners. It holds glue well, however, and does not let base colors, designs, or overlaps show through. It comes in sheets of about 28" x 18" and is very expensive up to 10 times the cost of Varese paper.

WALLPAPER

Wallpaper can be used in paper crafting, although it is usually very thick, which makes it most suitable for large projects such as wardrobe boxes. It can be difficult to fold, and overlaps are very noticeable because of its thickness. Make sure you purchase the proper glue for your particular type of paper. Before using wallpaper for any project, be sure to test the glue, folds, and overlaps. Wallpaper is available in single rolls of about 30 ft. x 20" and double rolls of about 60 ft. x 20". The cost of different wallpapers can vary considerably, depending upon the style and manufacturer.

PAPER AMOUNTS

Beginners should use a single type of paper and cloth at first. A purchase of 10 sheets* of paper and 1 yd. of cloth will yield a set of 5 or 6 attractively coordinating items. Listed below are the amounts of paper required for common projects; always buy a few extra sheets in case of mistakes.

- Medium-size flat binder: 2 sheets
- Copybook-size binder: 1 sheet
- Copybook-size journal: 1 sheet
- Expanding file: 1 sheet
- Shoe box: 2 sheets
- Hinged box: 2 sheets

*Handmade paper comes in sheets measuring 8 1/2" x 11" and up. The instructions in this book assume large sheets about 28" x 18".

KRAFT PAPER

Kraft paper is the stiff brown paper used for wrapping postal packages. It has very limited uses in paper crafting, primarily for reinforcing spines.

BOARD

Cardboard is the base for all paper craft projects. Each board will be completely covered with paper and cloth, so you might as well use grey board, which is usually the least expensive.

Board is available in bookbinding and art supply stores in sheets approximately 26" x 38" and in varying thickness. Be sure to use board appropriate to your project; very thick boards are suitable for large books and boxes but would overwhelm smaller projects. A particularly thin, lightweight board used to make book spines and round or oval boxes is called spine board. If you start with three sheets of board 0.059" (1.5 mm) thick, 0.098" (2.5 mm) thick, and one sheet of spine board, you will have enough to make 5 or 6 medium-size projects.

0.118" (3 mm) thickness is for large boxes and letter holders over 12".

0.098" (2.5 mm) thickness is for small boxes and letter holders up to 12".

0.071" (1.8 mm) thickness is for flat binders, journals, and albums over 10".

0.059" (1.5 mm) thickness is for flat binders, journals, and albums up to 10".

Spine board is used for the backs of journals and for round boxes.

CLOTH

Cloth is an important element in paper crafting. Its main purpose is to protect corners and edges from wear and tear; it is also used to reinforce seams and spines. Cloth is also a decorative element. Corners, fore edges, spines, coverings, and linings must all coordinate in color and scale, so choose the cloth for your project only after the paper has been selected.

The cloth used in paper crafting is a special bookbinding fabric sold in grades from A to F; the thicker D, E, or F cloth is usually called buckram. Bookbinding cloth is made of cotton, or a cotton–linen blend, and backed by a very thin layer of paper, which reinforces it and makes it sturdy to work with. Bookbinding cloth will not buckle, and glue will not seep through it. One yard of cloth will make about 5 or 6 projects.

GLUES

WHITE GLUE

All-purpose white glue can be used for adhering paper and cloth. It is readily available in craft and hobby shops but can vary greatly in viscosity. It will flow properly if diluted with water to the consistency of yogurt; a brush should leave slight bristle marks as it spreads the glue. Ready-to-use glue is available at bookbinding supply shops in jars of 40 oz., which is enough to make at least 20 projects.

CONTACT CEMENT

Contact cement is used to join pieces of board to make angled items such as boxes, trays, and letter holders. It must be spread on both of the surfaces to be glued together and then allowed to set for a few seconds before the surfaces are joined. Once the pieces have been positioned, press firmly. The glue sets immediately and repositioning of the pieces is no longer possible after they are joined, so be especially careful. If the basic structure of your project is even a little bit askew, adding a covering will not make it look any better.

RIBBON

Ribbon is used in paper crafting as ties for folders and hinged boxes, as pulls for tray inserts, and as grips for set-in box lids. Purchase only cloth ribbon, such as satin or grosgrain, which is available in fabric and notions stores in many different colors and widths. When choosing ribbon, make sure it is appropriate for the scale of the project and that the colors of the paper, cloth, and ribbon look well together.

TOOLS AND EQUIPMENT

For amateur paper crafting, you don't need a special work space or expensive, professional tools. A table and the items listed below are all you really need. To protect the table from cuts, use a sheet of thick board or a self-sealing synthetic cutting mat. Synthetic mats are more expensive than cardboard, but they last a lot longer.

FOR CUTTING

UTILITY KNIFE
Use a sharp utility knife for cutting paper, board, and cloth. Choose a knife with a blade at least 1" wide that can be adjusted in length and which retracts completely and safely into the knife handle. Especially handy is the snap-off type of blade, which is made of segments; when the blade tip becomes dull or nicked, you can break it off to create a fresh, sharp tip.

SCISSORS
Scissors are used for small finishing cuts. For all other cuts use a utility knife.

DRAFTING TRIANGLE
A drafting triangle is used primarily as a cutting guide in paper crafting, so it must be made of metal to prevent it being nicked by the blade of the utility knife. Use the triangle to measure, mark, and cut straight lines and angles. A 30-60-90 drafting triangle with a ruler on it works best.

FOR GLUING

PAINTBRUSHES
Flat paintbrushes work best for applying glue. Use brushes 1/2" – 2" wide, depending upon the size of your project.

FOLDING TOOL
The folding tool is a flat, rigid machined implement with a tip that may be rounded or sharp. It is used to stick paper and cloth into spots that are hard for fingers to reach. The folding tool can be purchased in craft shops and bookbinding supply stores. Remember to keep yours scrupulously clean at all times.

ADDITIONAL EQUIPMENT

A well-stocked paper crafting tool kit will include the following additional items.

BLOTTING PAPER
For absorbing moisture from the glue while the pieces are drying under weights.

SANDPAPER
For smoothing away any defects on the board; also for leveling out the joining of two or more pieces of board.

NEWSPAPER
For covering and protecting work surfaces from glue.

WEIGHTS
For holding glued items in place during drying; books, rocks, or other heavy items can be used.

SPONGE
For wiping glue from your fingers; always keep the sponge clean, moist, and handy.

CLEAN CLOTH
For gently rubbing over paper just glued in place, to make it adhere evenly and eliminate any air pockets.

TOOL MAINTENANCE

IN GENERAL
Equipment works best when it is clean and functioning properly. There are only a few rules to remember.

UTILITY KNIFE
Always use a fresh blade.

PAINTBRUSHES
Wash brushes thoroughly after use to prevent glue from drying on the bristles.

FOLDING TOOL
Remove any traces of glue on the tool by wiping it with a cloth or very fine sandpaper.

HANDS
Make sure hands and fingers are clean, dry, and free of glue.

GENERAL DIRECTIONS

WORKING WITH BOARD

DETERMINING THE GRAIN DIRECTION *Board is made up of fibers, and the direction of the grain is that in which the majority of the fibers run. Folding and cutting are easier along the grain. For flat binders and journals to close well, the board must always be cut along the grain.*

To determine the grain direction, hold a sheet of board in your hands and first try to bend it crosswise.

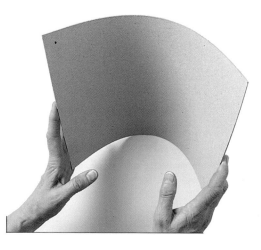

Then try to bend it lengthwise.

Whichever fold was easier to make was along the grain, and all cutting should be done in that direction.

The long side edges of spines should run parallel to the grain.

CUTTING THE BOARD

Use a utility knife and drafting triangle for accurate cuts.
- Place the board on your work surface.
- Position the drafting triangle on the corner of the board and align the sides of the triangle with those of the board; if the sides of the board are not perfectly straight, trim away excess board as needed.
- When you mark measurements on board, make small nicks with the knife blade. Do not use a pencil because a pencil line always has a thickness to it, which will affect the actual cutting dimensions.

The knife blade must not protrude from its sheath by more than 1/2" during cutting. In fact the shorter the blade, the steadier the cut.

- Place the unsanded side along the nicks already made.
- With one hand hold the drafting triangle firmly on the board.
- Hold the utility knife with the other hand and, keeping it perpendicular to the board, go over the cutting line a few times until the blade sinks into the board.
- Go over the cutting line again and again until the board has been completely cut through. The two pieces of board will separate by themselves. Never tear them apart, because that will create uneven edges. The cutting blade of the knife must always be perpendicular to the surface being cut so that the side edges are at right angles to the board top.

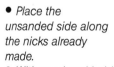

To make smooth, regular edges, always sandpaper them lightly after the board has been cut. Roll the sandpaper around a wooden block for use.

GLUING THE BOARD

When joining pieces of board, always note the grain direction and curve of the board.

The concave side of all boards should face inward.

This positioning helps when joining together the pieces of a box; it also facilitates the flat fastening of binders and book covers.

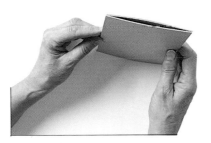

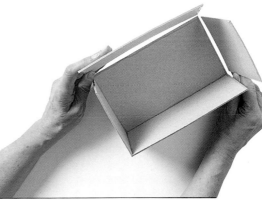

Contact cement is the glue used for joining pieces of board.

Spread it evenly on both surfaces to be stuck together, using a spreader or small piece of board. Do

not use too much glue or it will show through, even when covered with paper.

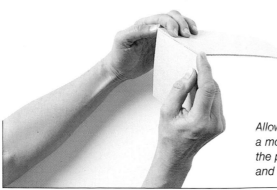

Allow the glue to dry a moment, position the pieces together, and press hard. Use

sandpaper to smooth any unevenness that might have occurred during joining.

CUTTING AND WORKING WITH PAPER

Paper, like board, has a grain. When glue is spread on paper, the paper tends to swell along the grain. During drying the paper usually returns to its original size. This swelling and shrinking can create a buckle in the board,

so place the covers under some weights to dry.
Cut paper with a utility knife and drafting triangle, the same as for cutting board. Make sure the blade of your utility knife is always fresh, to prevent tearing.

Light pressure is enough for an even cut.
Never use scissors for cutting out paper, because it will more than likely create rough edges. Use scissors for small finishing cuts only.

GLUING THE PAPER

Use white glue, properly diluted (see page 11).
Your work surface must always be scrupulously clean. It is a good idea to work over several layers of newspaper so that you can discard the top layer

as soon as it is soiled. When spreading the glue, use a brush appropriate to the surface to be covered. The brush must always be of good quality and clean. Any loose bits of dried glue or bristles will be visible under the

paper.
Dip the brush into the glue, then spread it from the center of the paper outward and over the edges.
If the paper is large, work quickly to prevent the glue on it from drying.

Position the paper on the board, then adhere it by repeatedly pressing outward from the center.
Use a clean cloth, but do not rub for too long.
Be careful to stick the paper very well near the edge of the board

before folding it under, to prevent air bubbles. Should any bubbles occur, however, or should there be an excess of glue, fix it at once: Pierce the bubble or excess glue with a pin, then press the surrounding area lightly until the

bubble or excess glue disappears.
When gluing paper onto cloth, do it with a steady hand. Glue leaves indelible marks on fabric, so after paper has been positioned, it cannot be moved without creating a mess.

CALCULATING THE SWELLING

Before cutting paper it is important to calculate the degree of swelling it will undergo when moistened by the glue, and to take this into consideration when measuring. This is particularly important when using different paper

sections need to meet perfectly.
For Varese paper, swelling of about 1/8" per sheet is considered normal. Remember that the paper swells mostly along the grain. Different types of paper swell differently. When using a new type of paper for the first time, always test it before calculating the measurements.

To calculate paper:
● Cut a 7 1/2" square of paper and an 8" square of board.
● Spread glue on the back of the paper.
● Stick the paper to one corner of the board with the edges aligned.
● Measure the paper horizontally and vertically.
You will notice that one measurement is now a tiny bit longer than the other.

Note the new measurements on your sample.
Keep your samples and note on them any new observations made while working. For the projects in this book, the measurements given were calculated based on a medium amount of swelling.
For perfect results, always test your papers.

CUTTING AND WORKING WITH CLOTH

Cloth for bookbinding (and for all other purposes) is made of horizontal and vertical threads that meet at right angles. The cloth must always be cut on the grain, which means parallel to the direction in which the threads run. To cut cloth, use a utility knife and drafting triangle. Cut the spine cloth with the vertical grain parallel to the selvage.
The selvage is the border that on bookbinding cloth is not covered by backing paper and on which small holes are usually visible. The selvage must always be cut away and discarded.

Cloth tends to curl. To flatten it, grip the ends of a cut piece and run it along the edge of the table (paper side down).

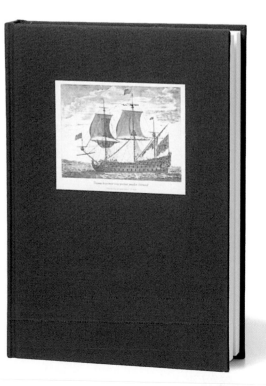

GLUING THE CLOTH

Follow the same instructions for gluing cloth as for paper.
• Use white glue.
• The work surface must always be perfectly clean.
• Spread glue outward from the center.
• Never rub the cloth with your hands, because it could become soiled or shiny.
If you need to apply pressure or to rub for longer than just an instant, cover the cloth with a sheet of clean white paper to avoid leaving marks.

TIPS AND TECHNIQUES

ASSEMBLING THE PIECES

After cutting out the boards, mark any imperfect sides with pencil. These marked sides could be used for the least visible parts of your project,

such as the hinge.

To make sure that both flat covers are identical, place one over the other on top of your work table.

The worst-looking edge should be reserved for the back of your project; mark that edge.

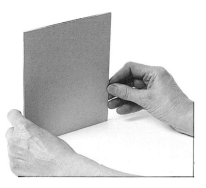

COVERINGS

Every sheet of hand-painted paper is unique; remember that when cutting.

Always mark the direction of the design on the back of the paper so that you will not need to check the direction continually during gluing.

*Fly-leaves for journals, albums, and copybooks can be made from the same paper used for the cover. Line the inside of each cover separately, using the method shown for the Self-Stand Frame (see pages 54–55).
If glossy, fine, or clear*

paper is used, make sure that the board on which it will be glued has no imperfections. These types of paper will

allow even the smallest defect to show through.

When covering boxes, first fold over the bottom allowances. You can then rest the boxes on your work table while folding over the top allowances.

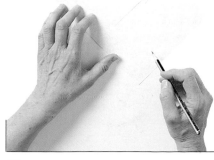

TESTING THE GLUE

Always check the thickness of the white glue before using it on your project. Dip a flat brush into the glue and pass it over a piece of paper. The brush should glide smoothly and its bristles should leave light traces. Where certain areas turn out too white, check to see if this is due to excessive thickness or just too much glue. Repeat this test, varying the dilution, until you achieve the desired effect. Prepare the glue with care, because it is one of the most crucial elements for creating satisfactory results.

COMBINING PAPER AND CLOTH

The edges of the paper to be glued over cloth must be perfectly cut because the contrast in color makes them really stand out. However thin the cloth may be, its thickness will always be visible when covered with paper, so keep the overlap of the two materials as narrow as possible, 3/16" (5 mm) or less.

Cuts in cloth must be particularly clean, with no unevenness, because even though hidden under the paper, the cloth thickness will still be visible.

A variation of the traditional method of covering with cloth and lining with paper is covering and lining completely with cloth, then applying shaped paper over the cloth. This is a more expensive covering method, but the result is elegant and no overlaps are visible. Another variation is to cover entirely with cloth and apply shaped paper over it, leaving the cloth corners and fore edges attractively visible.

RIBBON

Always buy good quality ribbons. Finish off one end of each ribbon with paper before applying the ribbons to your project so that you can prevent staining an almost finished project with glue and can work more easily. The ribbons are applied after the outer covering but before the inner lining. It is essential that the ribbon be inserted from the outside toward the inside to prevent the outer covering from lifting. Iron the ribbons when the project is finished. Attention to small details will pay off.

PICTURE FRAMES

The outer edges of frames will have a smoother look if the photo insertion slit is not visible. For a book-style frame, make each slit on the side facing the hinge.

With frames to be displayed on tables, such as the Self-Stand Frame, the photo slit should be at the bottom edge. To prevent the photo from shifting in the frame, wedge it in with a small piece of board.

A sheet of thin acetate can be inserted behind the opening to protect the photo. If you use glass, a deeper cavity will be necessary. Measure the thickness of the glass and increase the depth of the backing strips accordingly.

ROUND BOXES

The normal thickness of round box walls is equal to 3 thicknesses of spine board. If you want a box with stronger, thicker walls, or if the dimensions do not allow for making 3 rounds with a single strip of board, several strips will have to be joined together. To prevent the strips from fitting unevenly and creating an irregular edge at the box mouth, proceed as follows:

* *Prepare the board base and the strip for the walls (see page 129).*
* *Place the strip along the side edge of the base and wrap around it once.*
* *Turn the box upside down, so that the mouth of the box is on the table.*
* *Continue wrapping around the board. The strip will fit perfectly.*

If you intend to line the inside of the base with cloth, do this last, otherwise there is the risk of staining it with glue.

PENCILS

You can make matching paper-covered pencils to coordinate with a journal, pen-holder, or copybook.
• Cut a strip of paper as long as the pencil and slightly wider than its circumference.
• Spread glue on the back of the paper.
• Lay the pencil on the paper, aligning the unsharpened end with one short edge of the paper. Roll the paper around the pencil; secure the free end firmly.

ODDS AND ENDS

• When cutting out the various pieces of board, cloth, and paper for your project, indicate on the back of each piece where it belongs. This will speed up your work.
• Do not use felt-tip pens to mark fold lines on paper. Even if marked on the back, the ink will seep through and be visible.
• If you wish to make several of the same items, you can save time by preparing all the board pieces at the same time or have them cut to size in the store where you buy them. All of the paper and cloth pieces can be prepared beforehand too.

• Organize your work, and try to keep the measurements of the various objects of a set in scale. A number of covers could be made and then used for journals and copybooks as desired.
• If the board being used is thicker than 0.118" (3 mm), increase the fold allowances proportionally, because the board thickness takes up space.
• Make a note of the measurements of items you intend to make more than one of. Note also the details of particularly tricky steps and the various swellings for the papers used.

• Before spreading glue on the paper, always check the dimensions. Ridges on a book spine must be proportional to the size of the cover and spine. For a pocket journal, the ridges might be 3/16" (5 mm) wide; on a large photo album, they might be 5/16" (9 mm).

USING SEWING FABRIC AS BOOKBINDING CLOTH

Using sewing fabric in paper crafting can create all kinds of problems that will affect the finished results:
- They fray easily.
- The glue seeps through them.
- They lack consistency and stability.
To avoid these problems, you can back the sewing fabric with tissue paper to make it more similar to bookbinding cloth.

• Spread glue on the tissue paper.
• Place the fabric over the tissue paper and press firmly. Once it is dry, this backed sewing fabric can be used like any normal bookbinding cloth. If the fabric you intend to use is particularly heavy and does not lose its shape, the glue may be spread directly onto the board to be lined and the fabric placed over it. Always test your cloth.

TROUBLESHOOTING

CLOTH APPLIED ASKEW

Should you have applied a cloth covering somewhat crooked, it must be straightened out before proceeding to the lining phase. Mark the correct measurements on the cloth.

Place the drafting triangle on the new line and lightly pass the utility knife along it, scoring only the cloth.

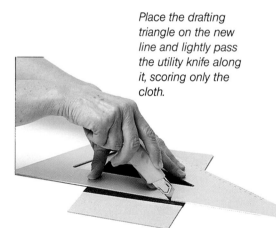

Cut the cloth all the way through and lift it away with the tip of the utility knife.

With the folding tool, smooth out the board from which the cloth was unstuck.

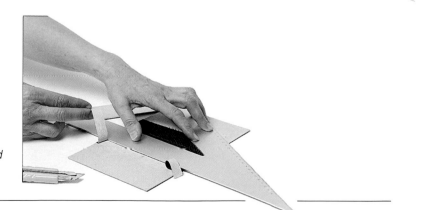

SEE-THROUGH CLOTH OR PAPER LINING

If lining is done with very thin or light-color paper, the overlap will show up clearly as extra thickness. To remedy this you must apply a compensatory piece to make the surface level.

If the covering paper is light in color, use a white compensatory piece to provide more luminosity. For journals it is a good idea to apply such pieces to the inside covers. These are always light colored and an inside compensatory piece can level off the fold-overs.

For the flat binder and covers with cloth corners, apply the compensatory piece to the outside.

For a perfect lining, apply the compensatory piece to the inside, too.

GLUE STAINS

Glue stains on paper, if still fresh, may be removed by dabbing them lightly with a damp cloth. This method usually works well with most types of paper.
Be careful with silky paper because the color could easily rub off.
If you happen to stain a piece of cloth with glue, don't attempt to clean it – you would only make the situation worse.

Unstick the cloth at once before the glue has set and apply a new piece. It is sometimes possible to cover stains with paper ornaments.

PROJECTS

FLAT BINDER

Difficulty: Medium
Time: 2 hours

The Flat Binder is one of the easiest paper craft projects to make. It consists of 2 pieces of board (called covers or flats) joined by a cloth spine that acts as a hinge. This binder includes the following features that you will incorporate into many other projects:
- Cloth hinge
- Cloth corners
- Ribbon ties

A flat binder is an excellent first project for beginners. The opportunities for creativity are endless, including the size, color, and type of coverings. The instructions below are for a flat binder that can hold about 20 sheets of typing paper.

Flos Solis maior

MATERIALS

Board, 0.059" (1.5 mm) thick
Bookbinding cloth
Covering paper, 2 sheets 28" x 18"
Lining paper, 2 sheets 28" x 18"
Ribbon, 2 pieces 1/4 yd.
White glue

RHODODENDRON SMITHII AUR

ROBINIA NEO-MEXICANA

MEASUREMENTS

BOARD, *0.059" (1.5 MM) THICK*
- *2 pieces 9 1/2" x 12 5/8", for the covers*

CLOTH
- *1 piece 4 3/8" x 13 3/4", for the outer hinge*

- *1 piece 4 1/2" x 12 1/2", for the inner hinge*
- *2 pieces 3" square, for the corners*

PAPER
- *2 pieces 8 1/4" x 13 3/4", for the outer coverings*
- *2 pieces 7 5/8" x 12 1/2", for the inner linings*

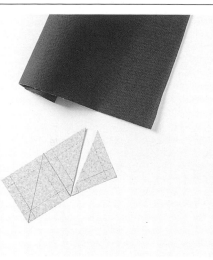

1 ATTACHING THE CLOTH CORNERS
Cut the 2 cloth squares in half diagonally to make 4 triangles.

On the back of each triangle, mark the fold lines with a pencil 5/8" from both short edges.

Spread glue on the back of one triangle.

Position one front corner of a flat cover on the glued triangle, aligning the board edges with the marked fold lines on the triangle; the cloth edges will extend beyond the board 5/8".

2

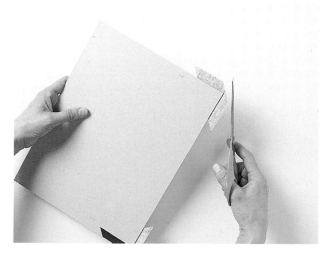

3 *Cut across the center point of the triangle with scissors; the remaining allowance should be equal to the board thickness plus a little more, which in this case is about 1/4".*

Fold over the right-hand allowance.

4

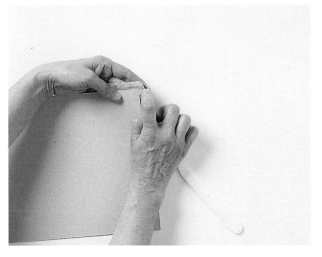

5 *Fold over the center tip of the triangle, pressing it in place with the folding tool or your fingernail.*

Fold over the left-hand allowance. **6**

7 *Flatten and smooth the cloth edges, using the folding tool.*

Repeat for the remaining 3 corners.

ATTACHING THE HINGE
On the back of the outer hinge, mark the following with a pencil:
- 5/8" for the upper fold allowance
- 5/8" for the lower fold allowance
- 3/8" for the center ridge **8**

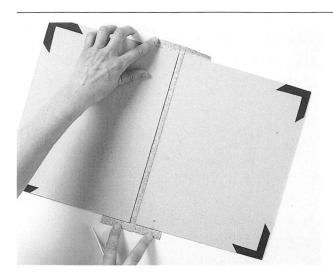

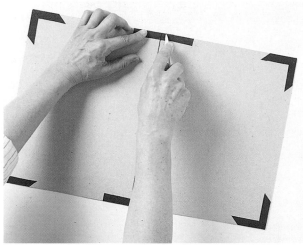

9 Spread glue on the back of the outer hinge, then position the two pieces of board on top, along the marked center ridge lines. Press in place firmly along the entire length of each board.

Fold over the top and bottom allowances, pressing the cloth deeply into the ridge. **10**

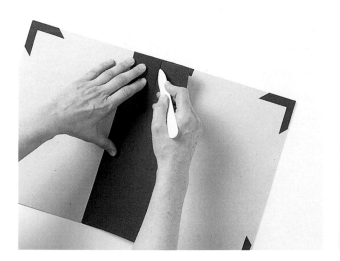

11 Apply glue to the back of the inner hinge. Position the left edge on the inside of the front cover, aligning it with the left edges of the top and bottom fold allowances.

While holding the right edge above the cover, press the left edge firmly in place, then press it deeply into the ridge with the folding tool.

Smooth the right edge of the inner hinge in place; press firmly.

The hinge is now complete and the 3/8" ridge is clearly visible. **12**

13 COVERING THE OUTSIDE
On each outer paper covering, mark fold lines on the back 5/8" in from both short edges and one long edge.

Position each board on a paper covering so that the allowance extends 5/8" all around. **14**

Make a center registration mark on the fore edges of the covers and the papers to make it easier to line them up again later.

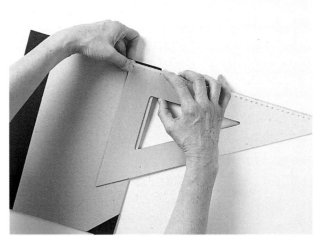

15 *Measure one cloth corner from the fore edge to the inner tip. Deduct from this measurement 3/8" for overlap. In this case, 1 3/4" – 3/8" = 1 3/8".*

Mark this calculated distance from the intersection of the allowance lines in both directions. **16**

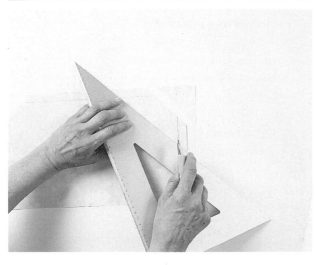

17 Align the drafting triangle with the points just marked, then use the utility knife to cut diagonally across the corners.

Spread glue on the back of the paper. Position the paper on your work table with the registration mark at the top. **18**

Position the open binder over the paper, aligning the edges and registration mark on the cover with the markings on the paper; press in place.

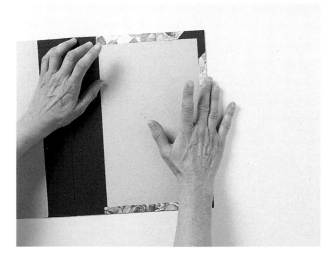

19 Fold up the allowances and press them firmly in place along the entire length of the board.

Cover the outside of the remaining cover in the same manner.

ATTACHING THE RIBBON TIES
Mark the location of the first ribbon tie halfway up and 3/4" in from the fore edge. **20**

Make a slit parallel to the fore edge and as wide as the ribbon by piercing at the mark; be sure not to let your blade slip or the damp paper will tear.

21 *Place one ribbon end over the slit and push it inside with the flat edge of the utility knife.*

Position the ribbon so that the short end faces the spine, the long end extends beyond the fore edge, and the entire ribbon is parallel to the top and bottom binder edges. **22**

23 *Apply glue to the short ribbon end, then press it firmly to the board with the folding tool to eliminate any bumps, because they would be visible after the lining was applied.*

Attach the second ribbon tie to the remaining cover.

LINING THE INSIDE **24**
Apply the first lining paper to the inside of one of the covers, positioning it 1/16" from the top, bottom, and fore edges of the cover; it will overlap the inner hinge by 3/16".
Repeat this procedure to line the remaining cover. Allow the binder to dry in an open position under evenly distributed weights for 5–6 hours between sheets of clean paper that will absorb the moisture of the glue.

25 FINISHING THE RIBBON ENDS

To prevent the free ends of the ribbon ties from fraying, you can cover them with the same paper used for the binder coverings.

Cut a paper rectangle for one end of each tie; the width should be three times that of the ribbon and the height about 3/4".
Fold the paper around the ribbon, then unfold it, and mark the fold lines with pencil.

26

Spread glue over the back of the paper, but not too much! You don't want the glue to seep through the paper.

Wrap the paper around the ribbon, so that the paper extends beyond the ribbon end a distance equal to the ribbon width; press flat.

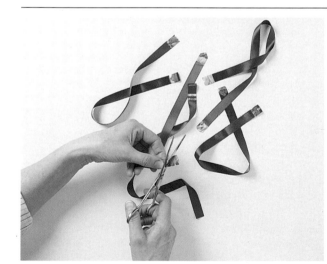

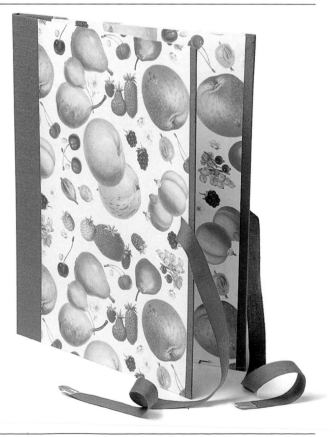

27

Allow the ribbon ends to dry thoroughly before shaping the paper tips.

Use scissors to trim the paper extensions beyond the ribbon ends to form a wedge, chevron, notch, curve, or other decorative shape.

BINDER-STYLE FRAME

Difficulty: Simple
Time: 3 hours

MATERIALS

Board, 0.059" (1.5 mm) thick
Bookbinding cloth
Covering paper, 1 sheet 28" x 18"
White glue

A binder is the simplest paper crafting project, and here it is combined with a frame, another simple and versatile project. The shapes and styles of the binder and frame offer lots of opportunity for you to be creative. You can fill your frames with photos, mirrors, treasured greeting cards, or needlework. Openings with straight edges are the easiest to cut and cover. If you wish to make frames with oval, round, or heart-shaped openings, it is best to buy a precut mat, because it is almost impossible to cut accurate curved shapes by hand. This project illustrates that in paper crafting a limitless number of different items can be created just by making slight modifications. Here we have created a binder-style frame by combining the techniques for both a binder and a frame.

MEASUREMENTS

BOARD, *0.059" (1.5 MM) THICK*
- 4 pieces 5 7/8" x 7 1/16", 2 for the covers, 2 for the frames
- 4 pieces 5" x 7/8", for the short frame backing strips
- 2 pieces 7 1/16" x 7/8", for the long frame backing strips

CLOTH
- 1 piece 2 1/2" x 8 1/4", for the outer hinge
- 1 piece 2 5/8" x 6 7/8", for the inner hinge

PAPER
- 2 pieces 5 3/4" x 8 1/4", for the outer binder coverings
- 2 pieces 5" x 7", for the inner binder linings
- 2 pieces 7 1/16" x 8 1/4", for the frame coverings

1 ASSEMBLING EACH FRAME
Mark a rectangular opening on the frame board 1 1/8" in from the edges.

Cut along the marked lines with the utility knife and remove the center cutout without tearing it; pass the blade over the lines as many times as necessary until the center comes out by itself.

Spread the frame backing strips with white glue, then position them on the frame, aligning the outer edges. Glue one long strip and then two short strips in place on the frame, leaving the fourth edge of the frame free for the photo insertion slit. **2**

3 *The space between the inner edges of the strips is the maximum photo size that will fit.*

Allow the frame to set and dry under weights for a few minutes.

COVERING EACH FRAME
Spread glue on the back of one of the paper frame coverings.

Position a frame in the center of the paper, with the strips face up; press hard.

4

5 *Cut across the tips of the paper corners about 1/4" from the board corners.*

Fold over the top and bottom allowances, making sure they stick securely to the strips.

Fold over and secure the tips of the paper corners as instructed on page 32.

Fold over the remaining allowances.

On the edge of the frame without a backing strip, stick the paper securely to the lower level of the frame between the upper and lower strips; use the folding tool or a piece of board; the paper will stretch the small amount needed to accommodate neat gluing.

6

7 Cut two diagonal slashes in the frame covering from corner to corner of the frame opening.

8 Fold over all 4 allowances on the paper, then cut away any excess from the tips that extend beyond the outer frame edges.

Allow the covered frame to set and dry under weights.

Cover the second frame in the same manner.

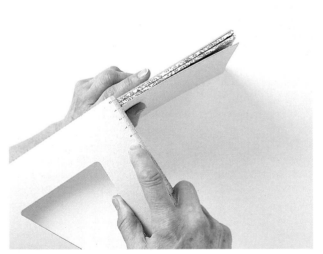

9 COVERING A ROUND OR OVAL OPENING
Purchase a precut mat and apply backing strips in the same manner as for the rectangular frame on page 40. To fold a paper covering over a curved mat opening, make a number of small snips with scissors through the allowance just to the edge of the board. The tighter the curve, the closer the cuts should be made, which will enable the paper to be folded around the curve without tearing.

10 ASSEMBLING THE COVER
Determine the width of the ridge in the hinge by placing the two covered frames on top of the two pieces of cover board, measuring the total thickness, and adding 3/16". For this project the ridge is 1/2".

Assemble the two cover boards and spine cloths to make a flat binder (see page 33).

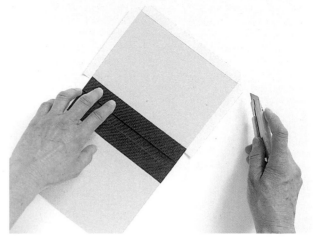

11 Mark the back of the covering papers for the outside of the binder 5/8" from both short edges and one long edge (see page 34).

Spread glue on the back of one of the marked papers.

Position one of the flat covers on top, aligning the board edges with the marked lines on the paper.

Cut across the tips of the paper corners about 1/4" from the board corners. **12**

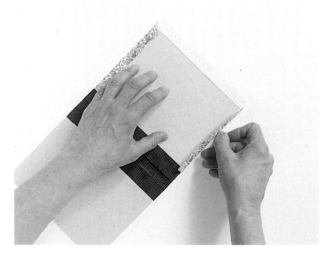

13 Fold over the top and bottom allowances, making sure they stick securely.

Use the folding tool to smoothly stick the paper at the corner onto the board. **14**

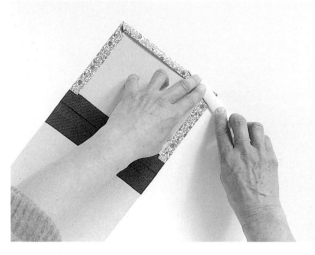

15 Fold over the allowance at the fore edge.

Flatten and smooth the overlapping allowances by pressing them with the flat edge of the folding tool.

Apply the paper covering to the remaining cover board in the same manner.

16 Apply the inner lining to the inside surface of each cover as directed on page 36.

17 ATTACHING THE FRAME TO THE COVER
Spread glue on the back of the two frame pieces, but only on the backing strips!

18 Open the binder with the inside face up.

Center a frame on the inside surface of each cover, aligning all of the outer edges; the photo insertion slit (the side of the frame with no backing strip) should face the hinge; press firmly.

19 *Insert a small piece of board into each photo insertion slit to prevent warping.*

Allow the open frame to set and dry under evenly distributed weight.

VARIATION: CONTRASTING FRAME
You can vary the colors and patterns of the inner spine and frame coverings.

20

21 VARIATION: CONTRASTING LINING
You can vary the colors and patterns of the inner linings of the cover.

VARIATION: CLOTH CORNERS
You can change the orientation of the binder by locating the spine on a short edge instead of a long one. Cloth corners can add a reinforcing and decorative touch, too.

22

GROUP FRAME

Difficulty: Simple
Time: 2 hours

The making of this frame is relatively simple and the effect is striking. The mat is a board with precut openings, which is available at craft shops and stationery stores. The width of the frame is proportional to the mat, so no measurements are provided for you. However, you will find algorithms for calculating the dimensions of the pieces so that you will be able to plan frames of all sizes.

MATERIALS

Board, 0.059" (1.5 mm) thick
Mat with multiple openings
Solid covering paper, 1 sheet 28" x 18"
Patterned covering paper, 2 sheets 28" x 18"
Self-adhesive hook
White glue

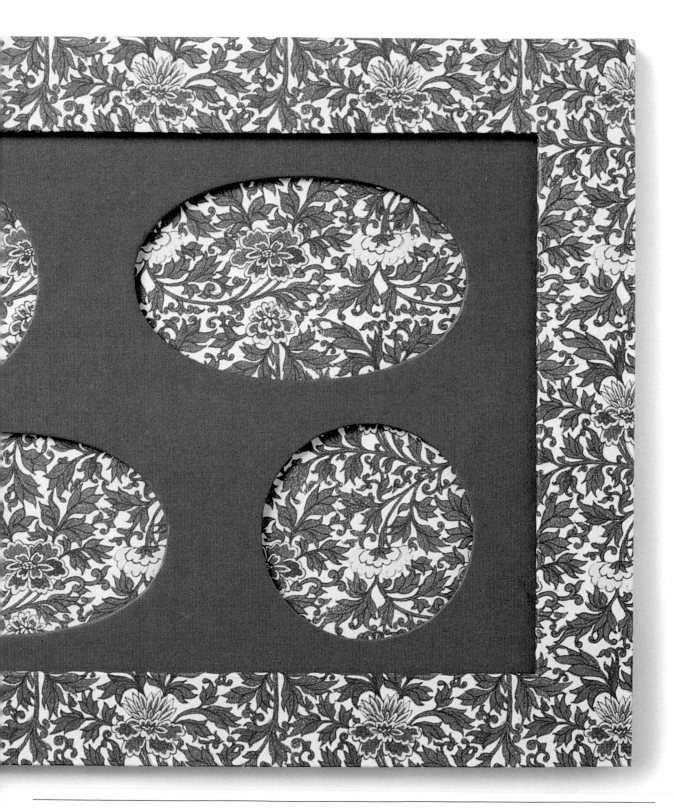

1 COVERING THE MAT
Cut the solid paper to the size of the mat, plus 5/8" on each edge for fold allowances.

Glue the solid paper to the front of the mat; fold the margins to the back.

Finish the inside edges of the mat openings as directed on page 42.

ASSEMBLING THE FRAME
Cut two pieces of board 3/4" longer and wider than the mat. **2**

3 *Cut out the center opening in one board to make a rectangular frame. The second board is the frame background.*

Cut 3 frame backing strips from another board, each 7/8" wide: cut 2 long strips and 1 short strip. Glue them to the back of the frame.

COVERING THE FRAME AND BACKGROUND
Cut 2 pieces of patterned paper the size of the frame plus 5/8" on each edge for fold allowances. Use one piece of paper to cover the frame. Use the second to cover the front surface of the frame background. **4**

Cut another piece of patterned paper a little smaller than the background board, then glue it to the back surface of the board.

5   *Glue the frame to the front surface of the background board, aligning all the edges (see page 44).*

Allow the frame to set and dry under evenly distributed weights

Slide the mat into the frame as you would a photo to test-fit it; remove the mat.

Secure photos as desired on the back of the mat so that they show through the mat openings, using the little corner stickers made for photo albums.   6

7   *Cut a fourth frame backing strip the same thickness and size as the short strip already in place. Cover it with patterned paper.*

Slide the strip into the photo insertion slit to seal it off and prevent the frame from warping.

Stick the self-adhesive hook onto the top center of the frame back.   8

SELF-STAND FRAME

Difficulty: Simple
Time: 1 hour

Now we are going to make a classic desk frame. The new feature introduced in this project is the two-piece self-stand that looks like a single piece.

MATERIALS

Board, 0.059" (1.5 mm) thick
Mat with precut opening
Bookbinding cloth
Covering paper, 1 sheet 28" x 18"
White glue

MEASUREMENTS

BOARD, *0.059" (1.5 mm) THICK*
For a frame with a round or oval opening, purchase a precut mat. The following instructions are for a frame 4 3/8" square.
• *1 piece 4 3/8" square, for the frame*
• *1 piece 4 5/8", for the frame background*
• *1 piece 4 5/8" x 2 3/4", for the base*
• *1 piece 4 3/8" x 3/8", for the long frame backing strip*
• *2 pieces 4" x 3/8", for the short frame backing strips*

CLOTH
The covering of the frame background and base is a single piece of cloth
• *1 piece 5 7/8" x 8 5/8", for the stand front*
• *1 piece 3 1/2" x 1 1/8", for the hinge*

PAPER
• *1 piece 4 1/2" x 4 5/8", for the back of the frame background*
• *1 piece 4 1/2" x 3", for the back of the base*
• *1 piece 5 1/2" square, for the frame*

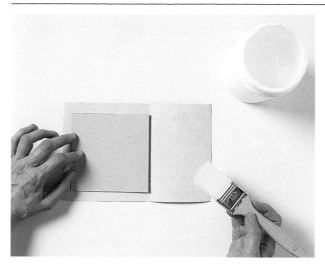

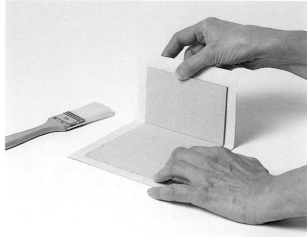

1 ASSEMBLING THE STAND
Spread glue over the back of the stand cloth. Place the large square board on top of one end of the cloth, leaving 5/8" for fold allowances on 3 sides; press firmly.

Position the base board so that it is perpendicular and adjacent to the bottom of the square board on the cloth.

Lift the free end of the cloth and adhere it to the upright piece of board.

2

3 *Lower the stand so that it is flat on the table, creating a ridge as wide as the board thickness.*

*Fold over the cloth allowances on all sides, finishing off the corners as instructed on page 43.
Push the cloth of the ridge inward with your fingernail, without tearing the cloth.*

Fold the base so that it is angled as desired.

4

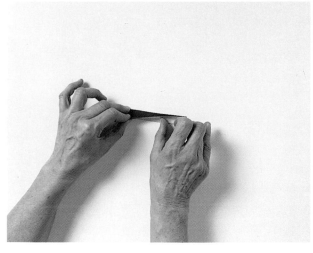

5 Fold the small cloth rectangle in half lengthwise with the cloth surface on the inside.

6 Spread glue over the papered back of the rectangle, then insert it into the fold between the two pieces of board, thus locking the stand into the desired angle.

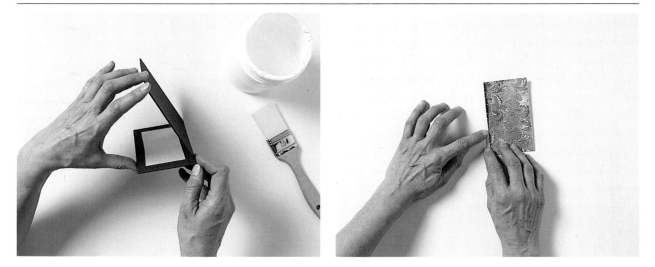

7 Allow the stand to dry, supporting it as needed so that it stays in the correct position.

8 Make a fold in the base covering 3/16" in from one long edge of the stand paper.

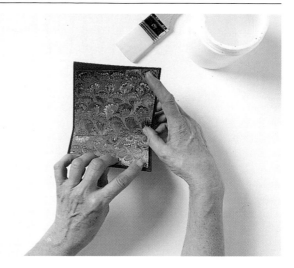

9 *Glue the paper onto the top surface of the base, aligning the fold with the joining of the two pieces of board.*

Glue the background paper onto the back surface of the background so that it overlaps the allowance on the base paper. **10**

11 ASSEMBLING AND COVERING THE FRAME
Make 3 backing strips for the frame with the round opening; then cover it with paper (see pages 40–42).

ATTACHING THE FRAME TO THE STAND
Glue the frame backing strips to the front surface of the background section of the stand so that the frame is centered and the photo insertion slit is at the bottom. **12**

Allow the frame to dry under evenly distributed weights that do not touch the stand.

RING BINDER

Difficulty: Simple
Time: 1/2 hour

MATERIALS

Board, 0.059" (1.5 mm) thick
Bookbinding cloth
Covering paper, 1 sheet 28" x 18"
Ring clasp
Grommets
White glue

A ring binder is very easy to make. The front and back covers are joined to the stiff spine with cloth. The ring clasp is sold in stationery stores and bookbinding supply shops. To fasten the rings to the spine, use grommets available in crafts shops. Use a grommet punch to make the holes and secure the grommets. It is a tool that costs very little and which will come in handy for many different types of projects.

A grommet punch is easy to use and ensures perfect grommets without ruined heads. Instead of purchasing a punch, you could ask your shoemaker to grommet for you. Do not, however, use a hammer!

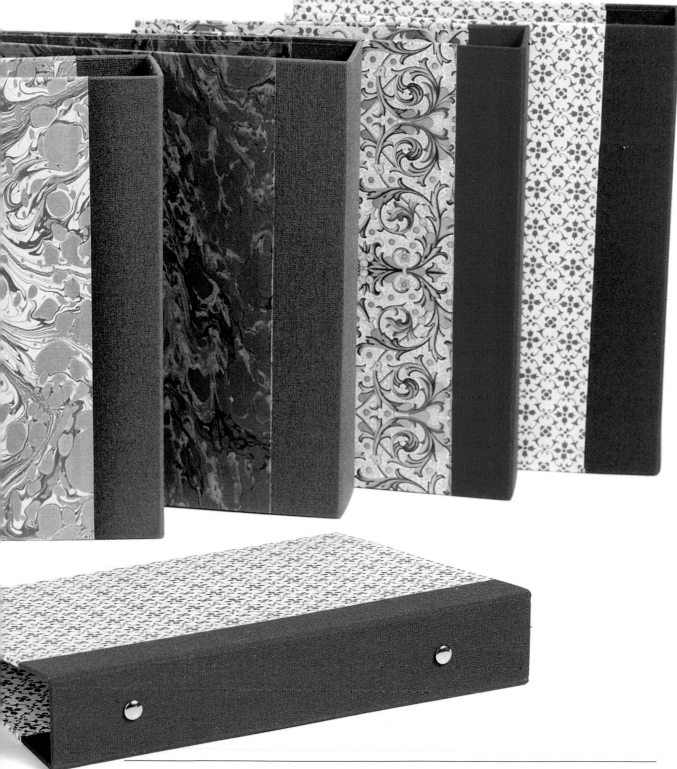

The ring binder, so practical and utilitarian, can become multipurpose depending upon what is kept in it. Stationery shops sell paper ranging from the simplest of white typing paper to the most elaborate of index pages, all of which come with prepunched holes. The binder can also be used to hold personal documents, recipes, photographs, and so on.

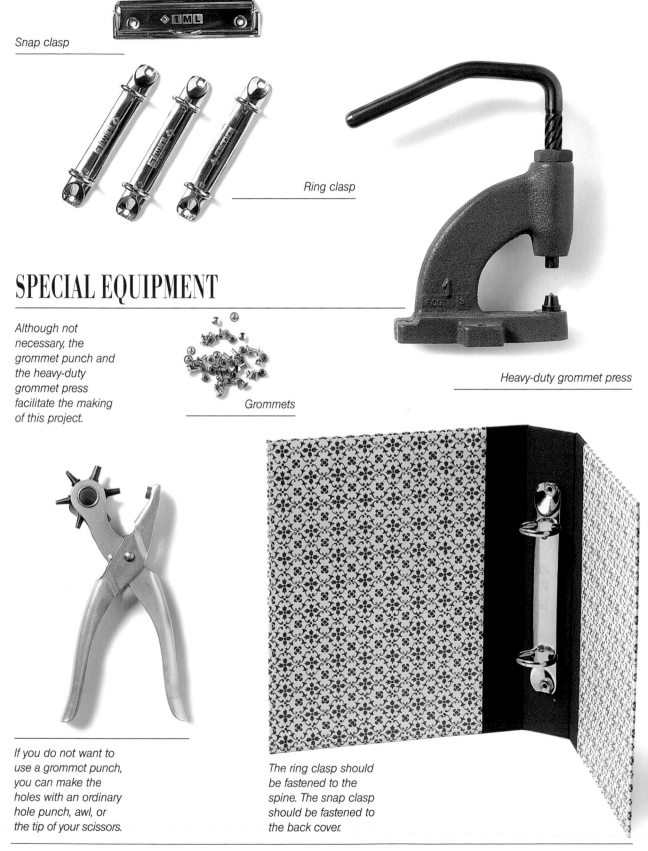

Snap clasp

Ring clasp

SPECIAL EQUIPMENT

Although not
necessary, the
grommet punch and
the heavy-duty
grommet press
facilitate the making
of this project.

Grommets

Heavy-duty grommet press

If you do not want to
use a grommet punch,
you can make the
holes with an ordinary
hole punch, awl, or
the tip of your scissors.

The ring clasp should
be fastened to the
spine. The snap clasp
should be fastened to
the back cover.

MEASUREMENTS

BOARD, *0.059" (1.5 MM) THICK*
- *2 pieces 6 1/4" x 7 1/2", for the covers*
- *1 piece 1 1/8" x 7 1/2", for the spine*

CLOTH
- *1 piece 4" x 8 5/8", for the outer spine*
- *1 piece 3 7/8" x 7 3/8", for the inner spine*

PAPER
- *2 pieces 5 3/4" x 8 5/8", for the outer coverings*
- *2 pieces 5" x 7 5/8", for the inner linings*

CUSTOM SIZES
If you wish to make a custom-size folder, remember the following:
- *The width of the spine is equal to the outer diameter of the rings plus 3/16".*
- *The width of the covers is equal to the outer diameter of the rings plus the width of the pages.*

1 ASSEMBLING THE COVER
Glue the spine board to the center of the outer spine cloth, leaving margins for the fold allowances.

Position a cover adjacent and perpendicular to one long side edge of the spine board. **2**

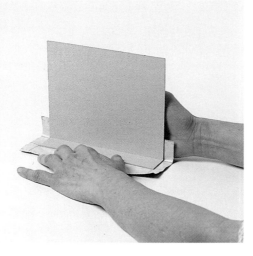

3 Raise the free end of the cloth behind the cover board and stick it in place on the back of the board.

Lower the cover so that it is flat on the table. Press the cover firmly into the cloth, creating a small ridge between the spine board and the cover board. The width of the ridge equals the thickness of the board. **4**

Attach the second cover to the spine in the same manner.

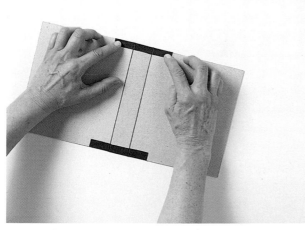

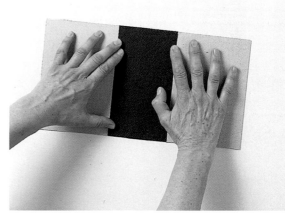

5 Fold over the top and bottom allowances; do not allow the cloth to sink into either of the ridges.

Spread glue over the back of the inner spine cloth, then position it flat without allowing it to sink into the ridges. **6**

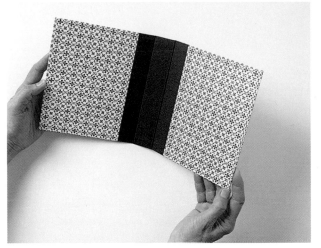

7 Before the glue dries, raise the front and back covers by 2"–2 3/8".

Run the folding tool or your fingernail gently along the rim of the ridge, making it adhere well without sinking into the ridge.

Close the binder and allow it to dry.

COVERING THE OUTSIDE AND INSIDE
Cover the outside surfaces of the front and back covers (see pages 43–44).
Line the inside surfaces of the front and back covers (see page 36).

8

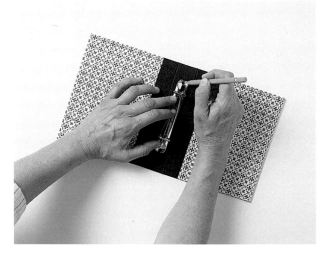

9 ATTACHING THE RING CLASP
Open the cover with the inside face up.
Position the clasp at the center of the spine and mark on the cloth the location of each mounting hole.

Make holes at each mark, using a grommet punch.

10

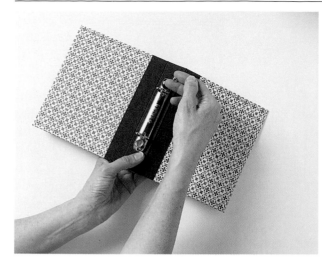

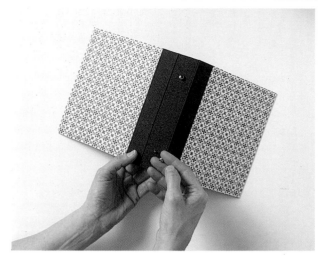

11 Insert the groove grommets from the inside to the outside of the spine through both the clasp and the board holes.

Apply the tongue grommets (with the round heads) to the outside; press hard. **12**

13 Place the spine on the grommet press with the clasp face down, inserting the tip of the press into the grommet hole; press to tighten.

VARIATION: SNAP CLASP
Instead of a ring clasp, you could choose a snap clasp. **14**

Place the snap clasp on the inside of the back cover where desired; make the holes and secure the grommets as described for the ring clasp.

EXPANDING FILE

**Difficulty: Simple
Time: 1/2 hour (for
the Open-Top File)
1 1/2 hours (for the
Covered-Top File)**

*These two projects
are super-easy to
make, but the results
are really impressive.
Buy the accordion-
fold expanding files in* *stationery,
bookbinding, or office
supply stores.
Assemble and attach
the covers and ties.
That's all there is to it!*

OPEN-TOP FILE

MATERIALS

Board, 0.059" (1.5 mm) thick
Covering paper, 1 sheet 28" x 18"
Expanding file, 10 7/16" x 6 1/16"
Ribbon, 2 pieces 12"
White glue

ABBIGLIAMENTO

MEASUREMENTS

BOARD, *0.059" (1.5 MM) THICK*
The grain direction is vertical (parallel to the short edges).
- *2 pieces 11" x 6 1/2", for the covers*

PAPER
- *2 pieces 12" x 6 1/2", for the outer coverings*

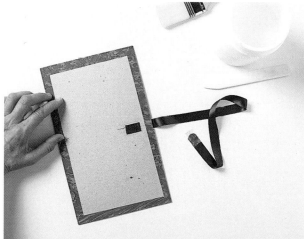

1 CHOOSING A FILE
Purchase an expanding file of the desired size and color.

2 ASSEMBLING THE COVER
Cover the outer surfaces of two pieces of board with paper, folding over the allowances on all 4 sides.

Attach the ribbon ties, positioning them 3/4" from the top edges of the front and back covers (see pages 35–37); finish the free ends of the ties as desired.

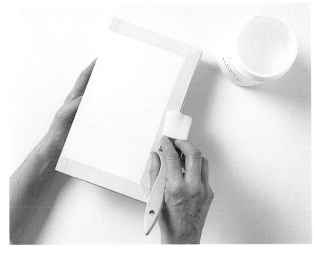

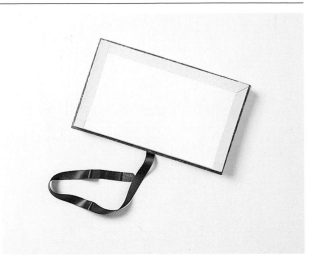

3 ATTACHING THE COVER TO THE FILE
Spread glue around the edges of one of the two outer surfaces of the expanding file.

Position the glued surface on the uncovered surface of a cover board, centered. **4**

5 *Glue the opposite outer surface of the expanding file to the second cover board in the same manner.*

To help the glue adhere, slide a few pieces of board into the expanding file and put it under weights. In this way pressure is applied to all four edges of the expanding file, instead of merely along the three thicker borders. **6**

COVERED-TOP FILE

MATERIALS

Board, 0.059" (1.5 mm) thick
Spine board
Covering paper, 2 sheets 28" x 18"
Expanding file, 10 7/16" x 6 1/16"
Ribbon, 2 pieces 12"
White glue

MEASUREMENTS

BOARD, *0.059" (1.5 MM) THICK*
- *2 pieces 10 7/8" x 6 1/2", for the covers*

SPINE BOARD
The grain direction is vertical (parallel to the short edges).
- *1 piece 10 7/8" x 14 3/8", for the rounded cover*
- *1 piece 10 7/8" x 6 1/2", for the front cover*

PAPER
- *1 piece 12" x 7 5/8", for the outside front cover*
- *1 piece 12" x 15 1/2", for the outside back cover*
- *1 piece 10 5/8" x 9", for the inside back cover*

ASSEMBLING THE COVER
Glue one 0.059" (1.5 mm) board to one end of the large spine board.

Allow to dry under weights.

1

2 *Glue together the other 2 boards – 0.059" (1.5 mm) board and the spine board – to make a board as thick as the one just assembled.*

Cover the outside of the second assembled board with paper, then attach a ribbon in the center.

3

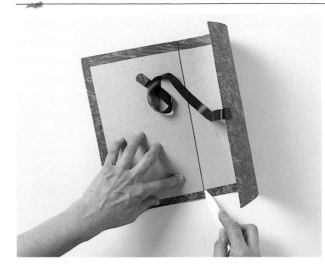

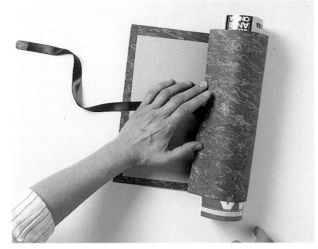

4 Cover the outside surface of the composite board.

Fold over all the margins and, with the help of the folding tool, make sure the paper adheres smoothly at the overlap.

Attach the second ribbon tie, placing it on the spine board 3/4" from the bottom front edge.

5 Allow to dry, folding the spine board around a sturdy can or tube in order to produce the curve about 3 1/8" deep.

6 Apply the inside back lining to the curved inside surface of the back cover.

7 ATTACHING THE COVER TO THE FILE
Join the 2 cover pieces to the opposite outside expanding file surfaces in the same manner as for the Open-Top File (see page 68).

JOURNAL

Difficulty: Medium
Time: 1 1/2 hours

MATERIALS

Board, 0.059" (1.5 mm) thick
Spine board
Bookbinding cloth
Covering paper, 1 sheet 28" x 18"
Body (pages only)
Kraft paper
White typing paper
Tailcap, 3 15/16"
Ribbon, for the bookmark
White glue

When we speak of making a journal, we really refer to making a book cover and then joining it to a purchased book body. Because journals can be made in all sizes, exact measurements are not provided for this project, but you will find algorithms to arrive at your own measurements. Following the directions for the journal, you can make photo albums, folders for receipts, index books, diaries, and copy books. The features covered in this project include the following:

● Spine
● Cloth fore edges
● Casing-in.

The journal cover is made up of two flat covers connected by a cloth spine. Inside the cloth spine is a support made of spine board and brown kraft paper.

The body of a journal usually comes without a bookmark or tailcap. In this project you will see how they are applied.

Classic book covers usually have cloth corners such as those on the flat binder. This project has cloth fore edges instead. You will note that the corners are still protected, but the appearance is totally different.

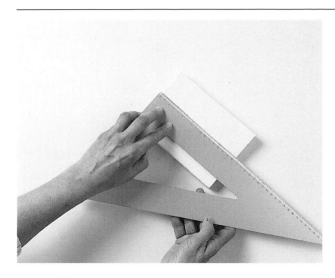

1 CUTTING THE COVER BOARDS
Measure the height of the body of your journal.

To this measurement add 3/8". The result is the height of your journal cover.

Measure the width of the body of your journal.

From this measurement subtract 1/16". The result is the width of your journal cover. 2

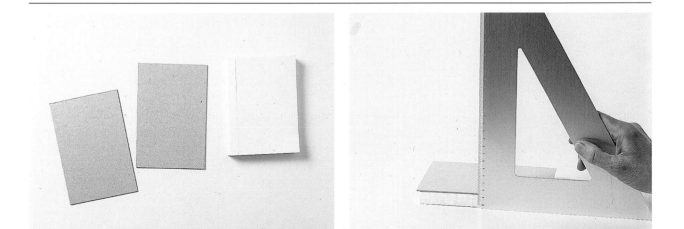

3 *Cut 2 boards for the front and back covers; the grain should run from top to bottom on each piece.*

MAKING THE SPINE
Place the body flat on your work table, then position the front and back covers on top of it. Measure the depth of the body plus the cover pieces.

The result is the width of the spine. 4

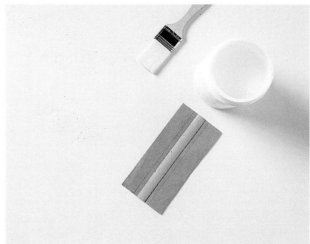

5 Cut the spine support from the spine board so that the grain runs vertically. The height of the support is the same as that of the covers; the width is the measurement from step 4.

6 Cut a piece of kraft paper the same height as the spine and the same width plus 2 3/8".

Spread glue over the concave inner surface of the spine. Position the spine, glue side down, at the center of the paper; press hard.

Mark a line on each side of the spine 1/4" from the board and parallel to it.

7 Spread glue on the exposed kraft paper. Position the front and back covers on each side of the spine, concave surfaces face down, aligning the inner edges of the boards with the marked lines on the paper; press hard.
To keep the top and bottom board edges lined up, check for level with the drafting triangle.

8 Decide on the amount of spine cloth to be left visible, then mark this distance as a vertical pencil line on the outside of the front cover. Draw a dash line 3/16" (5 mm) from the solid line.
The space between the two lines is the overlap allowance.

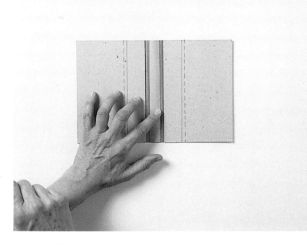

9 Open the cover on your work table, outside face up, and mark identical lines on the back cover.

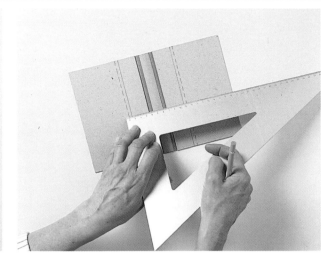

10 To determine the width of the spine cloth, measure the distance between the dash lines and to this measurement add 1/16", which the cloth will lose in width when it sinks into the ridges.

To determine the height of the spine cloth, measure the height of the covers and add 5/8" above and below for the fold allowances. Cut out the spine cloth along the grain.

11 Open the cover and position it on the table with the spine face up.
Spread glue on the back of the spine cloth and, keeping it well stretched, align one side edge of the cloth with one dash line so that the allowances extend equally above and below the covers.
Press the cloth edge firmly in place and be careful that the remainder of the cloth is elevated so that is does not stick to the spine.

12 Press the folding tool along the cloth and work it into the ridge, making sure it adheres well to the corners of the board.

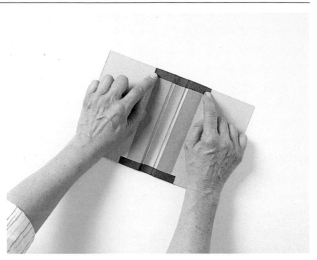

13 *Press the cloth onto the spine, then, again using the folding tool, work the cloth into the second ridge. Press well with the folding tool along all the corners of the board, lower the remaining cloth onto the board, and press hard.*

Turn the cover wrong side up and fold over the cloth, smoothing it but not allowing it to sink into the ridge. **14**

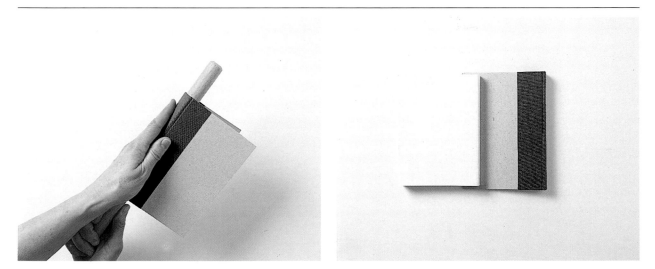

15 *To curve the spine, insert a large dowel or broom handle inside. Press hard from the outside with the palm of your hand so the spine board becomes more rounded.*

Remove the dowel, then close the cover and allow it to dry for 30 minutes with a small weight on the fore edge. **16**

Rounding the spine of the cover is necessary for photo albums and other thick books, but you can omit rounding for journals less than 3/4" thick.

17 ATTACHING THE CLOTH FORE EDGES

Decide on the width of the cloth fore edges and mark a solid line this distance away from and parallel to the fore edges of the cover on the outside. Measure inward toward the spine from the line a distance of 3/16" and draw a dotted line parallel to the solid one.

18

To determine the cut width of the cloth, measure the distance between the fore edge and the dotted line.

Multiply this measurement by 2, then add to the result the thickness of the board.

To determine the cut height of the cloth, measure the cover height and add 1 1/4" for fold allowances.

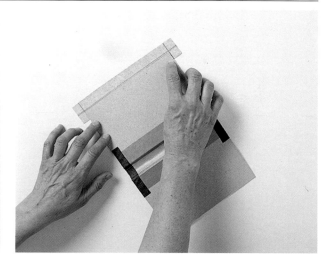

19

Use these dimensions to cut 2 strips of cloth; the grain should run lengthwise on each strip.

On the back of each strip, mark 2 parallel pencil lines at the widthwise center the same distance apart as the thickness of the board.

Mark top and bottom fold allowances of 5/8" each.

20

Apply glue to the back of the strip. Place one fore edge of the cover, wrong side up, along the nearest center line on the cloth, aligning the upper and lower edges with the marked allowance lines.

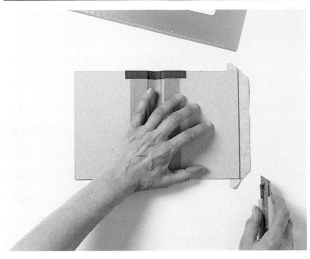

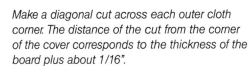

21 *Make a diagonal cut across each outer cloth corner. The distance of the cut from the corner of the cover corresponds to the thickness of the board plus about 1/16".*

Fold over the top and bottom allowances, then fold over the trimmed corners (see page 43). **22**

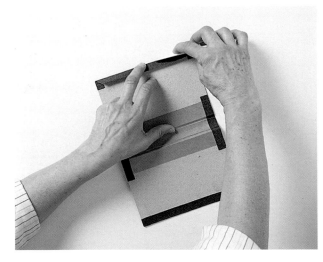

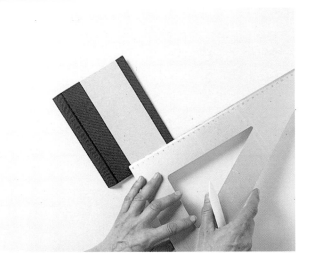

23 *Fold over the fore edge allowance; press firmly.*

Attach the second cloth fore edge to the remaining cover in the same manner.

COVERING THE OUTSIDE
*To determine the cut width of the paper, measure the distance between the cloth of the spine and one fore edge, then add to that distance 3/16" on each side for overlap.
To determine the cut height of the paper, add to the measured height of the cover 1 1/4" for the fold allowances.
Use these measurements to cut out 2 paper rectangles for the outer coverings.* **24**

25 Spread glue on the back of one paper and press it in place on the outside of the front cover, beginning with the overlap at the fore edge and working inward to the spine cloth.

26 Fold the top and bottom allowances to the inside of the cover; press firmly.

Apply the second paper to the back cover.

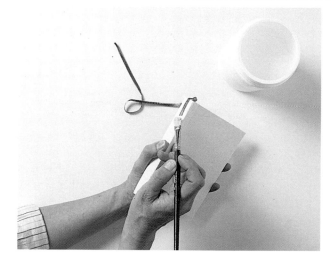

27 PREPARING THE BODY
Attach the bookmark by gluing 3/4" of one end of the ribbon to the spine on the outside of the book body.

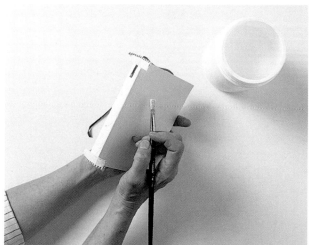

28 Cut a headcap and a tailcap a little wider than the spine.

Apply glue to the top and bottom of the spine.

Adhere the headcap over the bookmark and the tailcap at the bottom of the spine, so that the round, swollen part extends beyond the body.

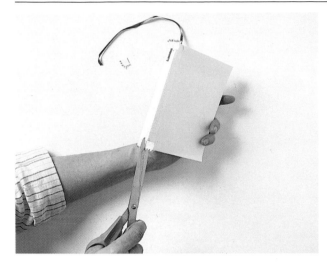

29 Allow the spine to dry. Cut the extension below the spine with the scissors; cut close to the spine.

30 To fasten the headcap and tailcap, cut 2 strips of typing paper 3/4" high and not much wider than the spine; glue them over the headcap and tailcap beneath the colored cord.

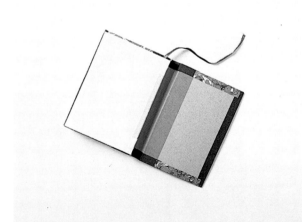

31 INSERTING THE BODY
Open the cover with the inside face up. Position the body of the journal on top of the front cover.

The cover will protrude 1/4" on the free sides. This margin is called the protruding edge of the cover.

32 To avoid soiling the journal with glue, place some clean typing paper between the first page (the fly-leaf) and the rest of the book, allowing the paper to protrude generously all around.

Spread glue on the inside of the front cover.

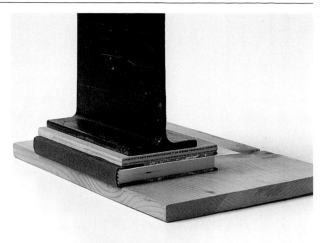

33 *Remove the protective typing paper, close the journal, then press firmly, not on the spine but on the cover only as far as the ridge.*

Turn over the journal and attach the body to the back cover in the same manner.

34 *To absorb the moisture of the glue, place a sheet of blotting paper under each cover. Position the journal on your work table so that the spine protrudes past the table edge. Place a piece of wood on the flat part of the cover. Place weights on top of the wood, which should extend as far as the ridge and not put any weight on the spine.*

Allow to dry overnight.

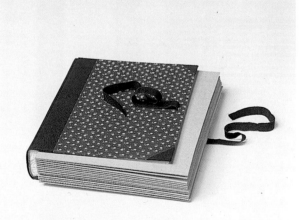

35 VARIATION: PHOTO ALBUM
Make the cover, then prepare the body and insert it in the same manner as for the journal.

36 *Before putting the album under a weight to dry, insert pieces of wood lath between the pages of the body so that the front and back covers are parallel.*

SHOE BOX

Difficulty: Simple
Time: 3 hours

The techniques used to make this project can be adapted to many other items that are structured like boxes, such as trays, drawers, and book sleeves.
The lid is the classic type used for shoe or wardrobe boxes. It is probably the most common and easiest to make. By changing the height of the lid walls, you can create different effects. To cover medium to large lids, each surface – inner and outer – is covered separately. The covering and lining of small lids are best applied as a single piece.

MATERIALS

Board, 0.098" (2.5 mm) thick
Covering paper, 2 sheets 28" x 18"
White glue
Contact cement

MEASUREMENTS: BOX

BOARD, *0.098" (2.5 MM) THICK*
- *1 piece 8 1/16" x 4 1/2", for the base*
- *2 pieces 8 1/16" x 3 15/16", for the long walls*
- *2 pieces 4 5/16" x 3 15/16", for the short walls*

PAPER FOR THE OUTER COVERINGS
- *1 piece 7 7/8" x 4 5/16", for the base*
- *2 pieces 8" x 5 1/8", for the long walls*
- *2 pieces 5 9/16" x 5 1/8", for the short walls*

PAPER FOR THE INNER LININGS
- *1 piece 7 7/8" x 4 5/16", for the base*
- *2 pieces 8 5/8" x 3 7/8", for the long walls*
- *2 pieces 8 5/8" x 3 7/8", for the short walls*

MEASUREMENTS: LID

BOARD, *0.098" (2.5 mm) thick*
- *1 piece 8 1/2" x 4 7/8", for the base*
- *2 pieces 8 1/2" x 1 1/8", for the long walls*
- *2 pieces 4 5/8" x 1 1/8", for the short walls*

PAPER FOR OUTER COVERING
The lid covering is a single piece that is cut big enough for covering the outside and inside of the walls.
- *1 piece 13 5/8" x 10 1/16"*

PAPER FOR THE INNER LINING
- *1 piece 8 1/4" x 4 5/8", for the base*

1 ASSEMBLING THE BOX
Arrange the box boards on your work table the way they will be assembled. Spread contact cement along the side edges that will be joined. Allow to set for about 20 seconds.

Join one long wall to the base, keeping it perfectly perpendicular. Next, add the 2 short walls. Finally, add the remaining long wall. 2

3 *You have now completed a basic box structure.*

Smooth away any unevenness with sandpaper. **4**

5 COVERING THE OUTSIDE OF THE BOX
Position the smaller papers on the short walls of the box. Press and stick the 3/8" fold allowances around the corners and onto the long walls.

At each top and bottom corner make a vertical slit in the allowance, cutting down to the board. **6**

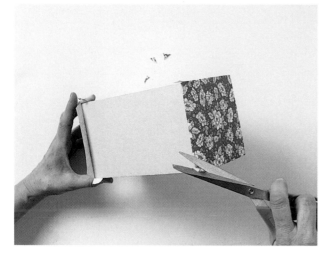

7 Snip across the bottom corners of the paper close to the box.

8 Press the bottom allowances in place on the base of the box.

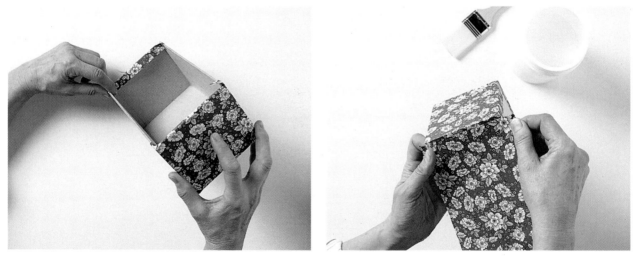

9 Fold over the top allowances.

10 Now position the long wall coverings, placing the paper a scant 1/32" from the corners and leaving 5/8" allowances at the top and bottom.

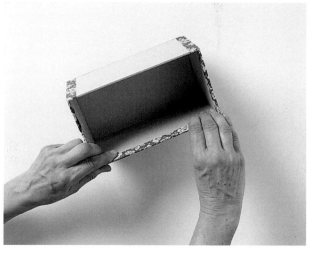

11 *Clip and press in place the bottom allowances.*

Clip and press in place the top allowances. 12

13 *Cover the base with the paper centered.*

14 LINING THE INSIDE OF THE BOX
Position a piece of lining paper on the inside of a long wall, allowing 3/8" to extend beyond each corner for fold allowance. Mark fold lines at the corners to facilitate positioning later.

15 *Spread glue on the back of the paper; position it inside the box, then press firmly.*
Apply the lining to the remaining long wall in the same manner.

Apply the linings to the short walls. **16**

17 *Apply the lining to the base.*

ASSEMBLING THE LID
Assemble the lid in the same manner as for the box. **18**

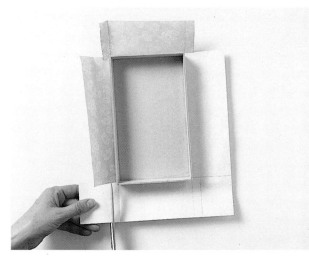

 19 COVERING THE LID
Spread glue on the back of the lid paper and position the lid on top of it.

Cut away the corners, leaving 3/8" fold allowance at both ends of each segment.

Lift and press in place the paper along the short walls; fold the side allowances over each corner of the long walls. **20**

Slit the fold allowances at the top corners.

21 *Fold the short wall coverings to the inside; press firmly.*

Lift and press in place the long wall coverings, first on the outside and then on the inside. **22**

Apply the lining to the inside of the base.

RECTANGULAR BOX WITH SET-IN RIM

Difficulty: Medium
Time: 3 hours

By modifying the Shoe Box so that it has a set-in rim, an attractive and elegant variation to the classic box can be created.

With the addition of the rim, the bottom of the lid meets the top of the outer box walls, and the box seals perfectly.

MATERIALS

Board, 0.059" (1.5 mm) thick
Board, 0.196" (5 mm) thick
Solid covering paper, 1 sheet 28" x 18"
Patterned covering paper, 2 sheets 28" x 18"
White glue
Contact cement

1 ASSEMBLING THE BOX AND LID
Assemble a box and cover the outside only (see pages 86–89).

2 *Assemble a lid the same length and width as the box, with walls 1 3/8" high.*

Cover the outside of the lid and the inside of the lid walls with the patterned paper (see page 91).

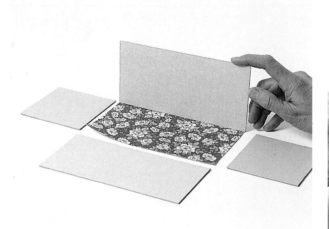

3 ASSEMBLING THE SET-IN RIM
Using the thinner board, make a box that fits snugly into the box from step 1. The walls must be taller than 1".

4 *Cover the outside with the solid-color paper, then line the inside with the patterned paper.*

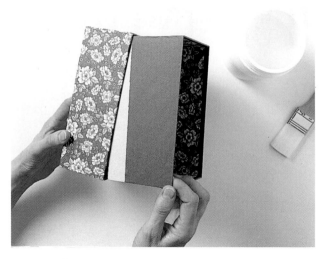

5 *Spread white glue over the inside of the base of the larger box and then insert the smaller box.*

Press against the walls and bottom of the inner box so that they adhere well to the surfaces of the outer box. **6**

7 *You have now made a box with an inner rim that adds stability to the box in an attractive manner.*

SQUARE BOX WITH SET-IN LID

Difficulty: Simple
Time: 1 hour

These boxes are very appealing when made in miniature. They make attractive and useful containers for candy, business cards, or jewelry. The set-in lid is easy to make. All it requires is an extra piece of board, glued to the underside of the lid, which fits inside the box and prevents the lid from slipping. The inner and outer coverings of small boxes can be made from one piece of paper, which speeds up the construction. Let your imagination run wild. Play with color and with the style of the lid grip. You can embellish the lid by adding a small arrangement of dried flowers or by inserting a piece of embroidery. The instructions that follow are for a small square box and 3 different set-in lids: one with a post and grip, one with a ribbon-loop grip, and one with an embroidered insert.

MATERIALS

Board, 0.059" (1.5 mm) thick
Covering paper, 1 sheet 28" x 18"
Round wooden toothpick and tissue paper,
for the post and grip
OR ribbon 1 1/2", for the loop grip
OR embroidery for the insert
White glue
Contact cement

SPECIAL EQUIPMENT

Grommet hole punch. It is useful but not essential.

MEASUREMENTS

BOARD, *0.059" (1.5 MM) THICK*
- *2 pieces 2 1/8" square, for the box bottom and the lid top*
- *2 pieces 2 1/8 x 1 3/8", for the long box walls*
- *2 pieces 2" x 1 3/8", for the short box walls*
- *1 piece 2 1/8" square, for the underlid*

PAPER
The covering of the inside and outside of the box walls is a single piece.
- *1 piece 9" x 3 3/8", for the covering and lining of the box walls*
- *2 pieces 2 1/8" square, for the box bottom covering and lining*
- *1 piece 3" square, for the underlid*
CLOTH
- *1 piece 3 1/8" square, for the lid top*

ASSEMBLING THE BOX
Assemble the box in the same manner as for the Shoe Box (page 86).

1

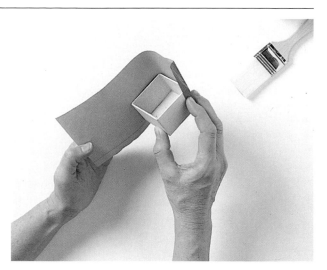

2 COVERING THE BOX
Because this box is small, the outside and inside walls are covered with a single piece of paper.

On the back of the largest covering paper, mark 3/8" fold allowances along one short edge and one long edge.

Spread glue over the back of the paper, then position it on the box, aligning the appropriate edges of the box with the marked lines of the paper.

Glue the side fold allowance around the corner onto the next wall, then glue and wrap the paper all around.

3

4 *Snip into the allowances at the top and bottom corners.*

Glue the bottom allowances to the base.

5

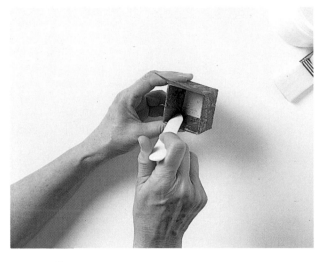

6 *Fold the top allowances to the inside. The paper will extend as far as the base plus a small overlap onto the base, on top of which the base lining will be applied.*

To make the paper adhere well at the inside corners, use the folding tool or a small piece of board.

Cover and line the base. **7**

8 ASSEMBLING THE LID
The set-in lid of this box is made of a lid and an underlid.

Before joining the two pieces, they must be covered separately; the lid is covered in cloth and the underlid in paper. Allow them to dry under weights.

Apply paper shapes decoratively to the top of the lid as desired.

To create a border, cut a square of paper 3/16" smaller than the lid and glue it to the center of the cloth-covered lid. **9**

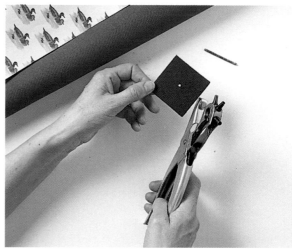

10 ATTACHING THE POST AND GRIP
Cut and discard the two sharp ends of the toothpick. Cut a strip of lining paper the same length as the toothpick. Spread glue over the back of the paper and wrap it tightly around the toothpick until the diameter is 1/8". Secure the end of the strip with a dot of glue.

11 *With the grommet hole punch, make a 1/8" diameter hole through the center of the lid, where the grip will be. Into this hole insert the covered toothpick.*

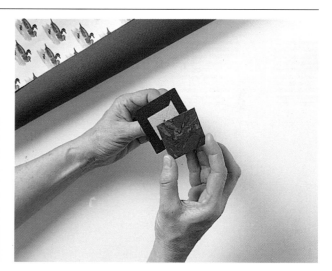

12 *Turn the lid over and trim away any part of the toothpick that extends below the underside of the lid.*

13 ATTACHING THE UNDERLID
Spread glue on the back of the paper-covered underlid, and center it on the underside of the cloth-covered lid; press firmly in place.

14 *Trim the toothpick so that it extends 3/8" or the desired distance above the lid for the grip.*

If the wood of the toothpick shows through, you can touch it up with a felt pen the same color as the paper.

VARIATION: SET-IN LID WITH A LOOP GRIP **15**
Make a slit into which the grip will be slid for attaching it to the underside of the lid (see page 35).

Fold the ribbon in half crosswise. With the blunt edge of the utility knife blade, push the ends of the doubled ribbon gently through the slit, allowing a loop to remain on top of the lid.

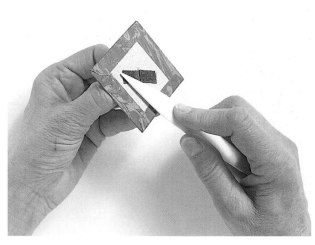

16 *Glue the free ribbon ends to the underside of the lid.*

Use the folding tool to flatten the thicknesses of the ribbon edges **17**

Glue the back of the underlid to the underside of the lid; the ribbon ends will be securely held between the 2 pieces of the lid and underlid.

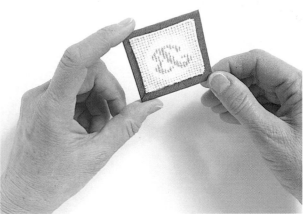

18 VARIATION: SET-IN LID WITH AN EMBROIDERED INSERT
Cut an opening of the desired shape in the center of the lid board, or use a small purchased frame.
Cover the lid as for a mat (see page 42).

Glue the embroidered cloth (smaller in size than the underlid) to the underside of the lid. **19**

20 *Glue a piece of tissue paper over the back of the embroidery; apply a drop of glue to each corner.*

Spread glue over the back of the underlid, then center the underlid on the underside of the lid. The embroidery will remain securely held between the lid and underlid.

BOOK-STYLE BOX

Difficulty: Medium
Time: 2 1/2 hours

MATERIALS

Board, 0.059" (1.5 mm) thick
Bookbinding cloth
Covering paper, 2 sheets 28" x 18"
White glue
Contact cement

The Book-Style Box is fitted between covers. Its name comes from its form, which resembles that of a book. The box and cover are made separately and then glued together. The cover has protruding edges on 3 sides. This type of box is very common in paper crafting. It can be made in any size and still maintain its stability.

MEASUREMENTS: BOX

BOARD, *0.098" (2.5 MM) THICK*
- *1 piece 7 7/8" x 5 1/2", for the base*
- *2 pieces 7 7/8" x 2 1/8", for the long walls*
- *2 pieces 5 5/16" x 2 1/8", for the short walls*

CLOTH
The lining of the outer walls of the box is a single piece.
- *1 piece 7 5/8" x 5 5/16", for the inner base*
- *1 piece 27 1/8" x 3 3/8", for the outer walls*

PAPER
- *2 pieces 8 5/8" x 2", for the long inner walls*
- *2 pieces 5 5/16" x 2", for the short inner walls*

MEASUREMENTS: COVER

BOARD, *0.059" (1.5 MM) THICK*
- *2 pieces 8 1/4" x 5 7/8", for the covers*
- *1 piece 8 1/4" x 2 1/4", for the spine*

CLOTH
- *1 piece 4 1/2" x 9 7/8", for the outer spine*
- *1 piece 2 3/8" x 7 5/8", for the inner hinge*

PAPER
- *2 pieces 9 7/16" x 5 7/16", for the outer coverings*
- *1 piece 8 1/16" x 4 3/4", for the inner lining*

1 ASSEMBLING THE BOX
Assemble the box in the same manner as for the Shoe Box (see page 86).

The outer lining of the walls is a single piece of cloth.
On the back of this cloth, mark the fold line 5/8" from one long edge.
Mark the side fold allowances at 3/8" from one short edge. **2**

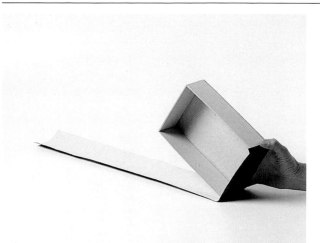

3 *Spread glue over the back of the cloth and position on top of it one short box wall, aligning the edges with the fold lines.*
Press the cloth firmly in place all around.
The free end of the cloth will overlap the already glued ends.
If the cloth swells slightly, trim it so that it does not extend beyond the corner.

Make vertical cuts in the fold allowances at the top and bottom corners. Fold the allowances and press firmly in place. **4**

Line the inside of the box with paper. A cloth margin of 3/16" will be visible at the top (see pages 89–90).
Apply the lining cloth to the inside of the base, gluing it directly onto the board.

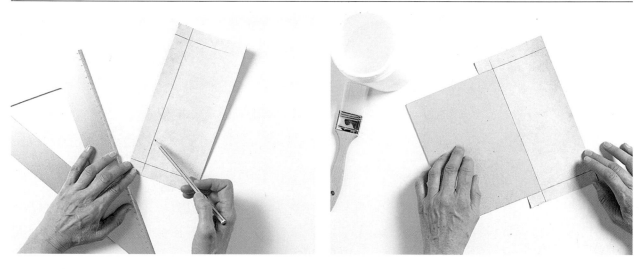

5 ASSEMBLING THE COVER
On the back of the cloth for the outer spine, mark a line 3/4" from each short edge for the fold allowance; mark another line 1" from one long edge.

Spread glue on the 1" allowance and position a flat cover on top, aligning the board edges with the marked lines on the paper. **6**

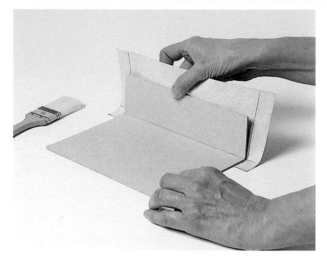

7 Spread glue on the center of the cloth, then position the spine board perpendicular and adjacent to the inner edge of the cover. Lower the spine board so that it is flat on the table.

Mark another line 3/16" from the long free edge of the spine board. 8

9 Spread glue over the remainder of the cloth and position on top of it the second flat cover, aligning the inner long edge of the board with the line just marked. You have just created a second, wider ridge that will give ease of movement to the lid hinge.

Fold over the top and bottom allowances; press the cloth into the wider ridge only. 10

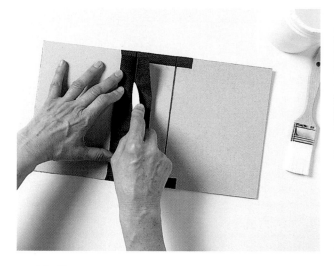

11 Glue the cloth for the inside of the hinge to the side of the wider ridge, aligning it with the fold allowances.
Finish off the ridge, sinking the cloth in well between the two pieces of board.

12 Apply the paper outer lining to each cover and fold over all of the allowances (see page 43).

At this point you could apply 2 ribbon ties, one for each cover (see pages 35–36), if desired.

13 Line the inside of the lid cover (the one near the larger ridge).

14 ATTACHING THE BOX TO THE COVER
Open the cover on the table with the inside face up.
Spread contact cement along the edges of the box bottom, and position the box on the unlined cover.
The long inner wall of the box should be 1/8" from the ridge. The 3 outer walls will be equidistant from the cover edges, creating protruding edges.

LETTER HOLDER

Difficulty: Advanced
Time: 3 hours

The challenge in this project is cutting out the shaped pieces. The features include the following:

- Base with protruding edges
- Divider.
Protruding edges can be used on boxes

and lids. Dividers can be used to create multisection trays or multidrawer chests.

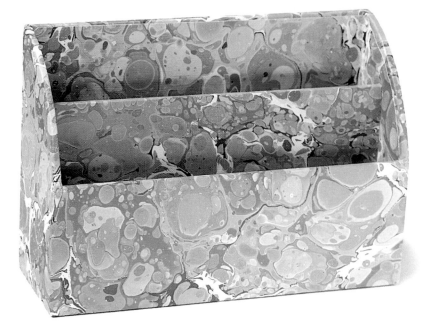

MATERIALS

Board, 0.059" (1.5 mm) thick
Board, 0.118" (3 mm) thick
Bookbinding cloth
Covering paper, 2 sheets 28" x 18"
White glue

MEASUREMENTS

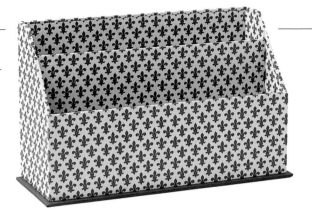

BOARD, 0.059" (1.5 MM) THICK
- *4 pieces 5 1/8" x 2 15/16", for the inner and outer side walls*

BOARD, 0.118" (3 MM) THICK
- *1 piece 2 3/4" x 8 5/8", for the front wall*
- *1 piece 5 1/8" x 8 5/8", for the back wall*
- *1 piece 3 1/8" x 8 5/8", for the bottom*
- *1 piece 4 3/8" x 8 1/2", for the divider*
- *1 piece 3 3/8" x 8 7/8", for the base*

PAPER FOR THE OUTER COVERINGS
When you cut out the paper for the front wall and 2 side walls, make sure that the designs will match at the overlapping points so that the seams are invisible.
- *1 piece 4" x 9 1/2", for the front wall*
- *1 piece 6 1/4" x 8 1/2", for the back wall*
- *2 pieces 4 1/8" x 6 3/8", for the side walls*
- *1 piece 3 1/8" x 8 5/8", for the base*

CLOTH
- *1 piece 4 1/2" x 10 1/4", for the upper surface of the base*

PAPER FOR THE INNER LINING
- *1 piece 2 5/8" x 9 1/4", for the front wall*
- *1 piece 5" x 9 1/4", for the back wall*
- *2 pieces 5 1/8" x 3 1/8", for the side walls*
- *1 piece 3" x 8 1/2", for the bottom*
- *1 piece 5 1/2" x 9 3/4", for the front of the divider*
- *1 piece 4 1/8" x 8 3/8", for the back of the divider*

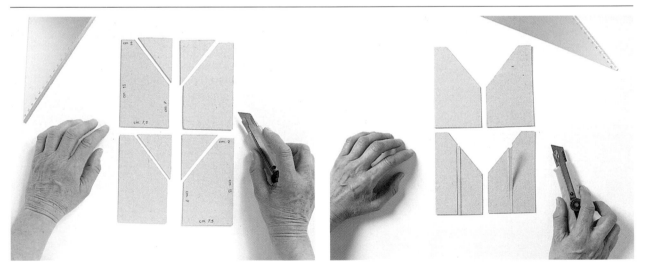

1 ASSEMBLING THE HOLDER
On the 4 thinner board rectangles, cut away identical triangles from one corner each.

On 2 of these shapes, cut out a 3/16" vertical strip at the center. **2**

3 Glue the small shapes to the larger ones so that there is a channel down the center of each for the divider.

The doubled pieces of the thinner board for the side walls are now the same thickness as the boards for the front and back walls.

4 Use one of the shaped side pieces with the channel as a pattern to cut the outer coverings for the side walls, adding 5/8" fold allowances to all of the edges.

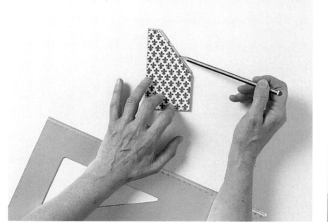

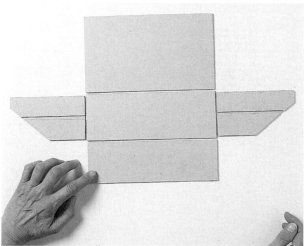

5 Use the side board to mark two same-size pieces on the lining paper. Cut them out, then trim away 1/16" from each edge of the paper.

6 Arrange the 5 pieces of board on your work table and join them as for the Shoe Box (see page 86).

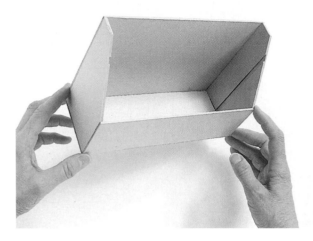

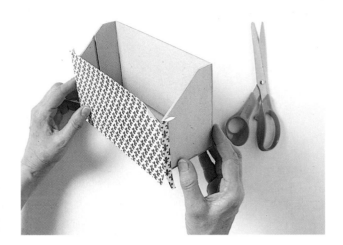

7 *You now have the basic box shape.*

COVERING THE HOLDER INSIDE AND OUT
Cover the outside of the front wall, adhering the fold allowances to the side walls.
Make 2 vertical slits and 2 set-in cuts in the allowances at the lower corners.
Fold over all the allowances.

8

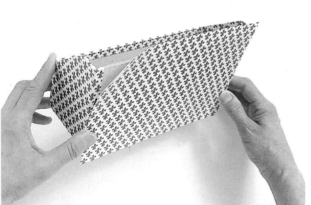

9 *Cover the outside of the side walls, positioning the paper 1/32" back from the front corner; glue the fold allowances to the back wall.*

Make a set-in cut in the bottom allowance in line with the back corner, and smooth out the front corner. Make a vertical slit in the top allowance in line with the back corner; make a perpendicular cut on the oblique side. Fold over all the allowances.

Position the outer covering for the back wall on the holder.
Round off the corners of the bottom allowance and glue it to the bottom of the holder, then fold the top allowance to the inside.

Line the inside of the long front and back walls, using the same technique as for the Shoe Box (see pages 89–90).

10

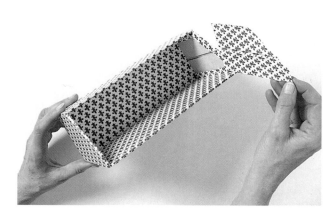

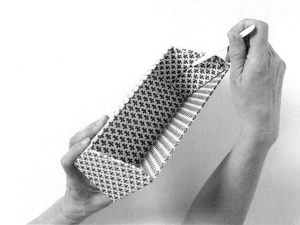

11 Test-fit the linings on the inside of the side walls.
Mark the channel sides with creases to help when positioning the linings for gluing.

12 Remove the side linings, spread glue on the back, then apply this paper to the inside of the box; use the folding tool to work the paper deep inside the channel.

COVERING THE DIVIDER
Cover the divider board completely.

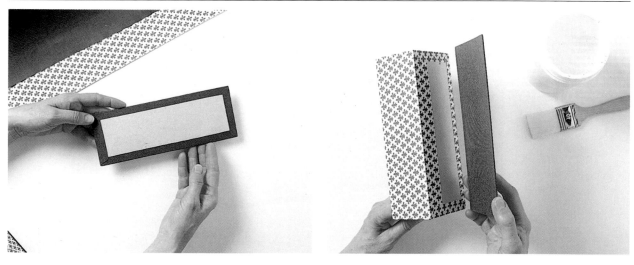

13 ATTACHING THE PROTRUDING-EDGE BASE
Cover one (top) surface of the base board with cloth.

Line the opposite (bottom) surface of the base board with paper. Allow to dry under weights.

14 Place the base on your work surface, cloth side up. Spread glue over the bottom of the letter holder and position it on the base so that the back edges are even and equal amounts extend beyond the holder on the other edges.

Allow to dry with evenly distributed weights inside the box.

HINGED BOX WITH TRAY

Difficulty: Advanced
Time: 4 hours

The Hinged Box has a tilt-back lid to which an underlid has been applied in order to give it more stability. All of the following features are incorporated in this project:
- Hinge
- Corners
- Cloth margins
- Underlid
- Ribbon ties
- Ribbon pulls

The box can include internal trays and dividers. Instead of the underlid, a mirror could be applied.

MATERIALS

Board, 0.098" (2.5 mm) thick
Bookbinding cloth
Covering paper, 2 sheets 28" x 18"
White typing paper
Ribbon, 1 3/8 yds.
White glue
Contact cement

MEASUREMENTS

BOARD, 0.098" (2.5 mm) thick
For the hinged box:
- 2 pieces 5 1/2" x 4", for the bottom and the lid
- 2 pieces 3 3/4" x 2 3/4", for the short walls
- 2 pieces 5 1/2" x 2 3/4", for the long walls
- 1 piece 5 1/8" x 3 1/2", for the underlid
- 2 pieces 3 3/4" x 1 3/8", for the tray supports

For the tray:
- 1 piece 5 1/8" x 3 1/2", for the bottom
- 2 pieces 3 3/8" x 1", for the short walls
- 2 pieces 5 1/8" x 1", for the long walls

CLOTH
- 1 piece 7" x 1 3/4", for the outer hinge
- 1 piece 5 3/8" x 2", for the inner hinge
- 2 pieces 4 1/8" x 3/4", for the corners
- 1 piece 7" x 1 3/4", for the lid fore edge
- 1 piece 5" x 3 3/8", for the inner bottom of the tray

PAPER FOR THE OUTER COVERINGS
- 1 piece 5 3/8" x 3 3/4", for outer hinge
- 1 piece 5 1/4" x 4", for the front wall

- 1 piece 5 3/8" x 3 1/8", for the back wall
- 2 pieces 4 1/8" x 4 1/8", for the short walls
- 1 piece 7" x 3 1/2", for the lid

PAPER FOR THE INNER LININGS
- 1 piece 5 3/8" x 3 3/4", for the bottom
- 2 pieces 6 1/4" x 2 1/2", for the long walls
- 2 pieces 3 3/4" x 2 5/8", for the short walls
- 1 piece 6 1/4" x 4 3/4", for the underlid

PAPER FOR LINING THE TRAY
The outer sides are lined with a single piece of paper. The inner bottom is lined with cloth.
- 1 piece 5" x 3 3/8", for the outer bottom
- 1 piece 17 3/4" x 2 1/8", for the outer walls
- 2 pieces 5 3/4" x 1", for the long inner walls
- 2 pieces 3 3/8" x 1", for the short inner walls

RIBBONS
- 2 ribbons, 9 7/8", for the ties
- 2 ribbons, 11 7/8", for the pulls
- 1 ribbon, 9 7/8", for the tray grip

1 ASSEMBLING THE BOX
Arrange the 5 pieces of board for the box on your work table and join them as for the Shoe Box (see page 86).

Finish off the upper part of the corners by applying 2 little paper squares. Snip diagonally toward the inside of each corner and then glue down the allowances. 2

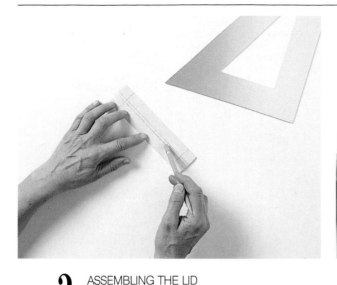

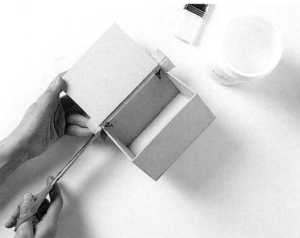

3 ASSEMBLING THE LID
On the back of the outer hinge cloth, mark the fold allowance lines 3/4" from the short edges. Mark a ridge 3/16" wide along the center.

4 *Spread glue over the back of the outer hinge cloth. Using the marked ridge lines as a guide, apply the hinge to the outside of the box and lid with the lid open.*

Make 2 cuts in the fold allowances up to the boards.

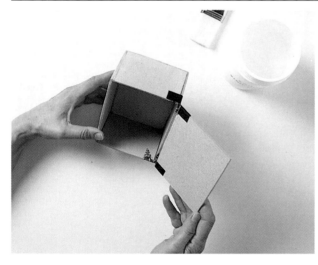

5 *Fold and glue the top and bottom allowances in place. Fold and glue the other 2 allowances to the lid, pressing along the groove of the ridge with the folding tool.*

6 *Fold the cloth of the inner hinge in half lengthwise (the paper goes on the outside). Apply glue and position the hinge at the center of the ridge, using the fold just made as a reference. Open the hinge and press hard with the folding tool to adhere the cloth to the bottom and to the sides of the ridge, gluing it also to the inner walls of the box and the lid.*

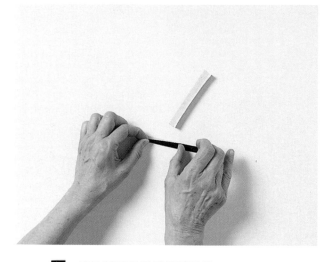

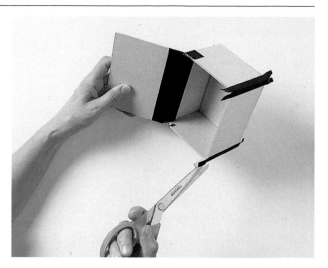

7 REINFORCING THE SEAMS
Fold one of the corner cloths in half lengthwise (with the paper on the inside) and press the fold to crease it.

Spread glue on the back of the cloth and apply it to one front corner seam of the box, leaving 5/8" at the top and bottom for fold allowances. Press firmly in place.

With the scissors make a vertical slit in the top allowance of the corner cloth and a set-in cut in the bottom allowance.
Fold over the 2 bottom allowances.
Fold the 2 top allowances to the inside, stretching them well and making sure that they do not create bulk at the corner.

Repeat for the second corner seam. 8

9 ATTACHING THE CLOTH FORE EDGE
Mark 2 parallel lines 1/16" apart along the center of the back of the fore edge cloth.

Spread glue and position the lid along the first line.
Make 2 diagonal slits and cut away the outer corners.

Fold over the side allowances to finish off the corners.
Now fold over the last allowance (see page 80). 10

11 COVERING THE OUTSIDE
Apply paper to the outside surface of the front wall so that the cloth corners are visible for about 1/16"–1/8" on each side; at the bottom and sides, leave 5/8" for each fold allowance. Round off the corners and press firmly in place.

12 On the paper for the first outer side walls, cut off the rectangle near the hinge.

The little rectangle to be cut off measures 5/8" x 3/4".
Cut the paper for the second outer side wall to be a mirror image of the first one.

13 Apply the first outer side wall covering. Place it 1/16" from the cloth corner, leaving 5/8" at the top and bottom and 3/8" on the back for the fold allowances.

14 Fold the back allowance to the back. Make a set-in cut in the bottom at the back corner; round off the back corner as for the front corner. Fold and glue the bottom allowances and then the top allowances.
Cover the second outer side wall in the same manner.

15 Position the paper for covering the outside of the back wall.

Smooth the bottom allowance, fold it, and glue it to the bottom.

16 To avoid soiling the box with glue, put a sheet of typing paper underneath the lid. Position the paper for covering the outside of the lid. About 3/16" of cloth will remain visible both from the side of the hinge and the cloth fore edge; 5/8" will protrude from every side for the fold allowances. Smooth the allowances and press them firmly in place.

17 ATTACHING THE PULLS
Glue one end of each ribbon pull to the inside of the side walls, up to 3/16" from the top of the wall.

Each ribbon should start at the bottom of one front seam and come out diagonally 1 1/8" from the back corner as shown.

18 ATTACHING THE TIES
Finish off one end of each ribbon with the covering paper.
Insert and glue the ribbons into the center of the front wall and the center of the lid at 5/8" from the edge (see pages 35–37).

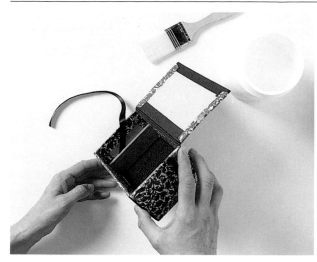

19 LINING THE INSIDE
First line the inside of the long walls (see pages 89–90).

Glue the 2 pieces of board, which will act as supports for the tray, to the inside of the short walls, positioning them at the bottom.

Position the 2 pieces of lining paper for the short walls; mark with creases the difference in levels created by the support boards. Keep an eye on the paper swelling, because the short inside wall linings must fit exactly without any overlap. **20**

21 *Spread glue on the back of the side wall linings and glue them in place.*
Line the bottom of the box.

Cover the convex side of the underlid. Allow it to dry under a heavy weight.

ATTACHING THE UNDERLID
Position the underlid on the underside of the lid and insert the ribbon pulls between the two pieces of board. **22**

23 *Pull the free ends of the ribbons to give the lid its proper angle, then secure the ribbons in place with spring-type clothespins.*

Remove the underlid and spread glue between the ribbons and the lid. **24**

25 *Remove the clothespins and cut away the excess ribbon ends.*

Spread glue on the back of the underlid and position it on the underside of the lid, centered. **26**

Allow to dry under a heavy weight, making sure the pulls don't get squashed.

27 ASSEMBLING THE TRAY
Assemble the tray in the same manner as for the box.
Cover the outside surfaces of the tray in the same manner used for the Book-Style Box (see pages 106–107.)
Line the inner surfaces in the same manner as for the Shoe Box (see pages 89–90).

Finish both ends of the ribbon tray grip. Spread glue along the center of the inside box bottom, between the short side walls. Place the center of the ribbon over the glue line and press it in place with the help of the folding tool.
One ribbon end will extend above each side wall to act as a grip. **28**

29 *Glue a piece of thin board over the ribbon so that the inner surface of the tray bottom will be all one level.*

Line the inside bottom of the tray with cloth. **30**

ROUND BOX WITH SET-IN RIM

Difficulty: Advanced
Time: 3 hours

Making curved forms presents the challenge of cutting and folding boards to fit. To make these shapes possible, use spine board which, being very thin, makes it easier to create round and oval items.

The method given below for the round box can also be used for oval boxes and for rectangular boxes with rounded corners. Stationery and bookbinding supply stores offer various sizes and shapes of board that can be used as box bottoms, lid tops, or bases. The

perfect seal of the lid on this box is achieved by making the box and lid to have the same diameter and by creating an inner rim. The set-in rim can be used with other shapes of boxes as well.

MATERIALS

**Board, 0.098" (2.5 mm) thick, or 2 board
circles 4" in diameter
Spine board
Covering paper, 1 sheet 28" x 18"
White glue
Contact cement**

MEASUREMENTS: BOX AND RIM

BOARD, *0.059" (1.5 MM) THICK*
- *1 circle 4" in diameter, for the base*

SPINE BOARD
- *1 strip 40 1/8" x 1 1/2", for the box wall*
- *1 strip 13 3/4" x 2", for the rim wall*

SOLID-COLOR PAPER
- *1 strip 12 7/16" x 2 3/8", for the outer rim covering*
- *1 strip 12 7/16" x 1 3/4", for the inner rim lining*

PATTERNED PAPER
- *The circle for the outer box bottom has the same diameter as that of the inner rim and the inside of the lid base.*
- *2 circles 4" in diameter, for the inner and outer rim bottoms*
- *1 strip 13 1/8" x 2 3/4", for the outside box wall*

MEASUREMENTS: LID

BOARD, *0.098" (2.5 MM) THICK*
- *1 circle 4" in diameter, for the base*

SPINE BOARD
- *1 strip 40 1/8" x 1", for the wall*

PATTERNED PAPER
- *1 circle 4 1/2" in diameter, for the outer base*
- *1 strip 13 1/8" x 2 3/8", for the outer wall*
- *1 circle 4" in diameter, for the inner bottom*
- *1 strip 12 3/8" x 3/4", for the inner wall*

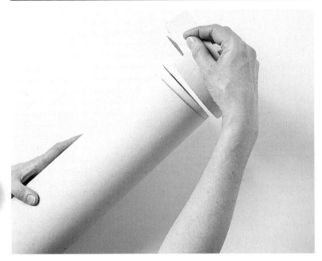

SPINE BOARD
Be very careful with the grain direction! If you cut the board the wrong way, it won't wrap around.
Make sure the grain runs parallel to the short edges of the strip.
If your spine board sheet is not long enough for cutting the walls, cut an additional strip and overlap the ends after grading them with sandpaper.

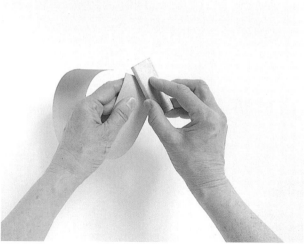

1 ASSEMBLING THE BOX
Cover the surface of the base board intended to be the inside with the paper circle.

Use sandpaper to grade both short ends of the spine board that will be the box wall. 2

3 *Apply contact cement around the side edges of the base board.*

Position the graded spine board along the side edges of the base board and wrap it all around, applying a drop of glue now and then. Continue wrapping in this way to make the 3 rounds necessary for a strong wall. Secure the free end of the spine board with contact cement. 4

5 *The assembly of the box is now complete.*

ASSEMBLING THE LID
Assemble the lid in the same manner as for the box.

6

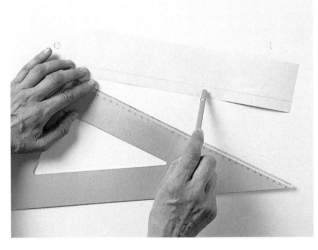

7 COVERING THE BOX
On the back of the outer wall covering, mark a line 5/8" from one long edge for the bottom fold allowance.

Spread white glue on the back of the paper. Position the box on the paper, matching the fold line with the bottom edge of the box. Roll the box along the line; press well with your hands, smoothing the paper in place as you go.

8

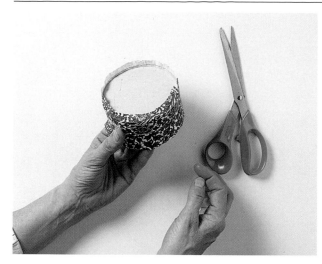

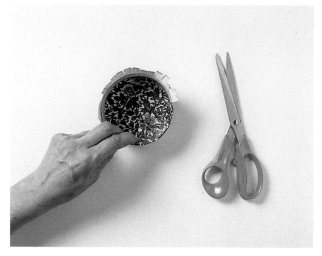

9 *Make vertical snips on the lower fold allowance as far as the board and 1/8" apart.*
The closer together you make the snips, the easier the paper will fold over the curved edges.
Fold the allowances over to the bottom of the box.

Make vertical snips on the upper fold allowance to within 1/16" from the board and about 3/8" apart.
Fold the upper allowances to the inside of the box.
Glue the outer bottom covering in place. **10**

11 ASSEMBLING THE RIM
Assemble the rim in the same manner as for the box and lid.

COVERING THE RIM
Use white glue to adhere the outer covering of the rim wall so that 3/8" extends above the top. **12**

13 *Fold the upper allowance to the inside. There is no need to snip the allowance before gluing because the board is very thin.*

Spread glue on the inner walls of the box. Insert the rim into the box and press it firmly in place.
Line the inside of the rim. **14**

15 COVERING THE OUTSIDE OF THE LID
Glue the circular lid covering in place. Make closely spaced snips into the fold allowance all around, cutting inward as far as the board. Fold over the allowances to the lid wall; press firmly in place.

Fold one edge of the paper for the outer wall 1".
Open the folded paper and spread a light layer of glue on the back. **16**

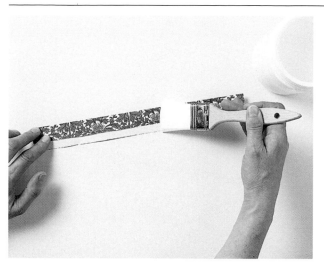

17 Fold the paper along the crease, then spread a second layer of glue over the folded strip.

Position the strip on the outer wall of the lid, aligning the fold with the lid top. At the bottom there should be a 3/8" fold allowance. Press firmly all around.
Make vertical snips to within 1/16" from the board; the snips should be 3/8" apart or less. Fold them smoothly to the inside of the lid. **18**

19 LINING THE LID
Spread glue on the back of the paper and line the inside walls.

IDEAS

Personalize your projects by making them unique. You can do this by experimenting with new types of paper, by playing with different colors and patterns, and by using different types of cloth. The inside of the hinged box with the wildflower theme is divided into sections and can be used as a sewing box.

In this very different type of box, there are 3 projects combined: the Frame, the Shoe Box, and the Letter Holder.

Tiny toys and other treasures can be stored in this hinged box with a charming bear theme.

Round and oval boxes can also have lids that fit like that of the rectangular Shoe Box. Attention to small details makes your boxes more special. The checked lip above the houses emphasizes the curves of the box, its roundness, and its flexibility. The solid-color cloth covering of the oval lid wall separates the simple rose paper pattern on the box and lid.

Keeping your paper napkins in order will no longer be a problem. Make this pretty napkin holder following the Shoe Box method and using two creatively shaped pieces of board for the long surfaces. The huge grosgrain bow is not typical of classic paper crafting, but we have included it anyway.

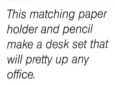

This matching paper holder and pencil make a desk set that will pretty up any office.

Collectable coins, stamps, or notions can be stored visibly in this plaid box with its transparent lid. The glass is held in place by frame backing strips. The box is covered in two steps: First, the frame is covered and the paper inside the opening is folded over. The glass is slid into place next, and the remaining strips of paper are folded over the outer edges.

Wallpaper borders have been applied to the outer walls and inner rims of these little boxes.

These elegant little boxes with set-in rims can be used to hold party favors, jewelry, or knick-knacks. The cloth-covered lids overlap paper-covered walls.

To finish off medium-size boxes, you could use wallpaper borders, cloth ribbons, and upholstery trimmings.

The inside bodies for photo albums are available in bookbinding supply shops in various styles and colors. The cover of the album below has a cloth spine and corners as well as a lively wallpaper outer covering.

The window effect on the album cover above has been obtained by making the front cover with two thinner pieces of board, one whole and the other with a precut window, similar to making a frame. The whole board was covered with cloth only at the location of the window. The cutout board was covered, the cloth folded over only at the center of the opening. The 2 pieces of board are joined, and then the cloth along the 3 edges is folded over.

Many different types of paper, including old magazine pages, can be used as coverings. To the front cover of this Book-Style Frame was glued an old advertisement that adds a touch of originality to the box.

To make a photo album that will stand out from the rest, make a stiff cover like that of the Flat Binder. The opening of the front cover is facilitated by a hinge. The inside pages of the body are held in place by a satin ribbon tied into an attractive bow at the front.

The classic stand-up frame looks different if a mat is inserted into the frame opening. Experiment with different types of paper, contrasting colors, and shapes.

The same photo, but this time embellishing the front cover of a ring binder used to hold old family letters.

You could insert a small piece of needlework or a photo into the lids of boxes and covers of books. You could in this manner personalize a photograph album with the name of a newborn child or decorate each party-favor box with the initials of its recipient.

This little chest of drawers was made from a structure like that for the Shoe Box, and the inner space is divided as for the Letter Holder. The drawers are really trays like those inside the Hinged Box that fit perfectly in the spaces created by the divider.

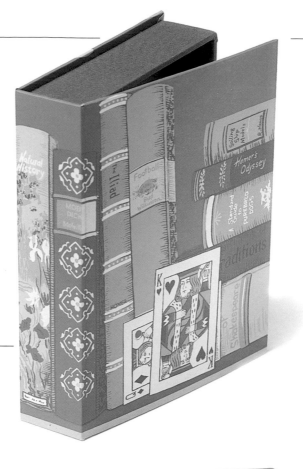

To cover this Book-Style Box, paper depicting old volumes was used. You could hide documents or other items inside the box and place it on your library shelf among the real books.

This chest of drawers could be used to hold letter paper and envelopes. By varying the number of the drawers and adapting the thickness of the board to the size of the box, you can create different types of chests.

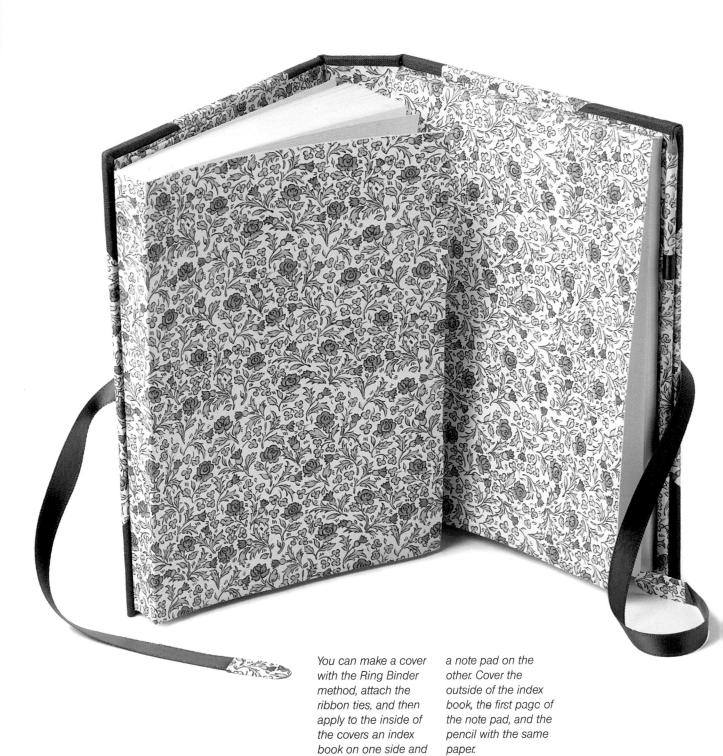

You can make a cover with the Ring Binder method, attach the ribbon ties, and then apply to the inside of the covers an index book on one side and a note pad on the other. Cover the outside of the index book, the first page of the note pad, and the pencil with the same paper.

This desk set features flowery paper, cloth corners and spine, and coordinating ribbon ties and lid grip.

The spine and 2 corners of this photograph album are made from reinforcing cloth.

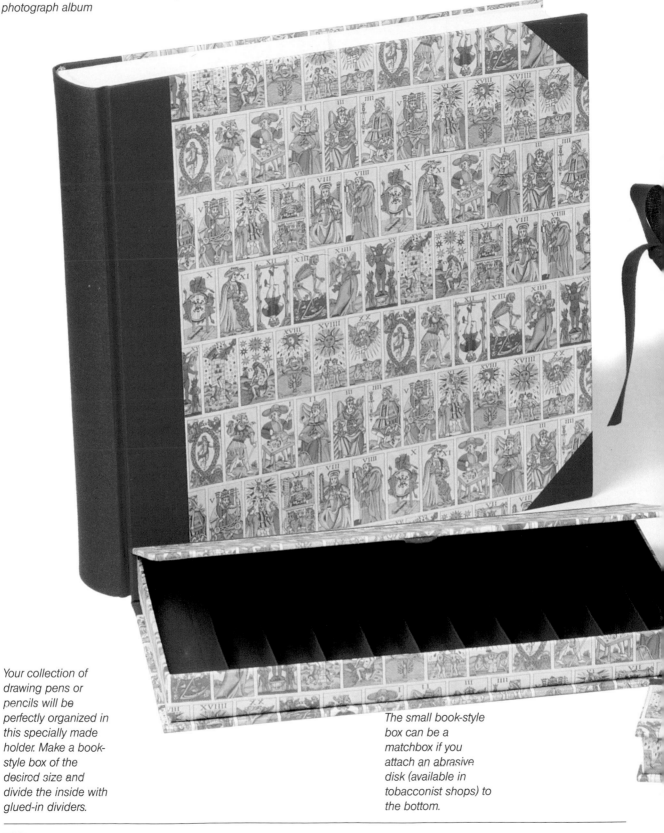

Your collection of drawing pens or pencils will be perfectly organized in this specially made holder. Make a book-style box of the desired size and divide the inside with glued-in dividers.

The small book-style box can be a matchbox if you attach an abrasive disk (available in tobacconist shops) to the bottom.

This flat binder is very easy to make in all sizes. The paper used to cover this particular desk set features rows of Tarot cards. The first board objects covered in paper that we know of were, in fact, boxes for playing cards, made in the 18th century.

The box with the set-in rim is appropriate for holding pretty stationery.

These pretty plaid covers are very original. While applying them, however, particular precision and attention are required. Bookbinding cloths are available in solid colors and different variations of colors; other types of cloth can be used only with careful handling.

Wardrobe boxes are very useful for organizing space. The plaid-covered box is accented with coordinating solid-color-cloth-covered lid walls. The box with stripes was completely covered in cloth. Each surface was then covered with paper, leaving only the cloth corner seams visible, which protects them from wear.

Boxes with set-in rims are very elegant and suitable for gift packaging. By varying the shapes and the proportions between the box and lid, very different effects can be achieved. One box might hold delicious chocolates or a bottle of liqueur. Thanks to the rim, the box closes perfectly, so you could also use it as a container for talcum powder. Add a powder puff the same color as the covering paper to use with the powder.

The covering of this pretty blue box is a special handmade paper known as starch paper. The name comes from the starch glue used in preparing the color.

The choice available among styles and colors of paper makes it possible to personalize all of your craft projects. Use contrasting or coordinating colors and patterns as desired.

This book-style frame can be used as either a traveling photo frame or a desk frame.

GLOSSARY

BODY The inside part of a book, excluding the cover, made up of pages only; also called a text block.

BOOKMARK A narrow cloth ribbon attached to the spine of the body of a book for marking individual pages.

CASING-IN The joining of a cover to the body of a book by gluing the endsheets to the inside surfaces of the covers.

CONCAVE The term for a board surface whose center recedes.

CONVEX The term for a board surface whose center protrudes.

COVER A protective enclosure or casing for the body of a book. It consists of a front and a back cover connected by a spine.

ENDSHEETS The first and last pages of the body of a book, which are glued to the inside surface of the front and back covers.

FLY-LEAF A loose page at the beginning or end of a book between thc body and the cover. It is not glued to the covers.

FOLD ALLOWANCE Extra covering material on the head, tail, and fore edges of a book cover, which is folded over the edge of the board and glued to the opposite surface.

FOLDING TOOL A machined piece of bone, ivory, wood, or plastic, typically 6"–12" long, 1"–1 1/2" wide, and 1/8" thick. The tip can be pointed or rounded, and the edges are tapered. It is used for folding paper by hand, working in ridges, and folding paper and cloth over board to adhere them to the opposite surface of the board.

FORE EDGE The opening edge of a book; the right-hand edge when a closed book is viewed from the front.

FRONT AND BACK COVERS Flat pieces of board that are connected by a spine or hinge to make up the cover of a book.

GRAIN
The pattern in which fibers line up in paper, board, and cloth.

GRAIN DIRECTION
The direction in which the majority of paper, board, or cloth fibers run. Cutting paper, board, or cloth parallel to the weft or warp without cutting the threads diagonally is called cutting along the grain. It is easiest to fold and cut along the grain.

HEADCAP and TAILCAP
The coverings at the top (head) and bottom (tail) of the spine of a book. They are formed by folding the covering on the spine over the head and tail and then shaping it.

HINGE
A strip of cloth (usually cotton or linen) that connects two pieces of board and forms a flexible joint.

PROTRUDING EDGE
A small margin on the cover of a book that extends beyond the head, tail, and fore edges of the body. It protects the pages.

RIDGE
A shoulder that is shaped into the side of a spine or hinge. On a book, the ridges are between the front and back covers and the spine; they enable the cover to open more easily. On a hinged-lid box, the ridge is between the lid and the wall it connects to. On a flat binder, the ridge is in the hinge between the two covers.

RIM
The tall set-in walls of a box over which the sides of a lid fit.

SELVAGE
A border on cloth that must be cut off and discarded; it may contain small holes, which are also cut away.

SPINE
The part of the inner body of a book where the pages are joined together. It is also the outer part of a book that connects the front and back covers.

SPINE BOARD
A slightly rounded board that forms the spine between the front and back covers of a book; it is also used to make round and oval boxes.

INDEX